School, Home, Community

You and Your Health
Teacher's Edition

Julius B. Richmond, M.D.
Elenore T. Pounds, M.A.

In consultation with
Orvis A. Harrelson, M.D., M.P.H.
Gladys Gardner Jenkins, M.A.
Wallace Ann Wesley, Hs.D.

Scott, Foresman and Company
Editorial Offices: Glenview, Illinois
Regional Sales Offices: Palo Alto, California •
Tucker, Georgia • Glenview, Illinois •
Oakland, New Jersey • Dallas, Texas

Highlights of *You and Your Health*

A deeply human approach

Opening chapter in each text centers on mental health.
Program emphasizes building of positive self-concepts; helps
   students understand themselves and others.

Easy for students to read and use

High-interest content, effective writing styles, and powerful
   visuals enhance readability.
Readability is at or below grade level according to Fry and
   Spache formulas.
Anatomical drawings are accurately done by a professional
   medical illustrator.

Easy to teach

Chapters organized for easy teaching and learning.
Helpful "Teacher's Notes" printed on pupil's pages in
   Teacher's Edition.
Chapters can be taught in any order. Books can be used with
   large or small groups or by individuals.
Behavioral objectives are posed directly to students.
Testing program is built into books.
End-of-Book test is action-oriented.

Learner verified

Scott, Foresman health materials have been widely used in
   the classroom. This new Program has evolved out of 30
   years of interaction among learners, teachers, and the
   publisher.
New materials have been classroom tested. Classroom teachers have served as advisors on the Program.

Unique provisions for school-home communication

School and Home feature at the end of each chapter.
Supplementary school/home *Activity Booklets* with parents'
   message on the back of each Activity Sheet.

Age-appropriate content written by health science experts

Content based on research about children's health and safety
   needs and concerns.
Double-checked for accuracy by experts in all areas of the
   health sciences.

ISBN: 0-673-11038-9

345678910 SEG 898887868584838281

Does Level Two cover concepts in those aspects of a complete health education program that are appropriate to seven- to eight-year-olds?

Mental Health, Human Relations, and Values Awareness	*Pages 8–29*
Personal Health, Fitness, and Dental Health	*Pages 74–113*
The Body, Human Growth and Development	*Pages 32–47, 78, 104–105*
Nutrition	*Pages 79–87*
Family Health	*Pages 29, 73, 86–87, 102–103, 113, 137, 161*
Prevention and Control of Disease, Health Services	*Pages 98–101, 114–137*
Drugs (Including Alcohol and Tobacco)	*Pages 60–63, 100–101, 108, 126–127*
Community and Environmental Health (Human Ecology)	*Pages 138–161*
Consumer Health	*Pages 84–87, 102–103*
Safety	*Pages 30–73*
Health Career Awareness	*Pages 67, 76–77, 100–101, 108, 116–134*

A guide to the Scope and Teaching Sequence of YOU AND YOUR HEALTH K-8 is available on request from Scott, Foresman and Company. This guide includes concepts and selected behavioral objectives.

Does it motivate children to apply what they are learning in health to their daily lives at school, at home, and in the community?
Pages 18–19, 29, 48–58, 60–67, 79–89, 98–99, 102–103, 106–107, 140–154

Does it present materials and approaches that include the family in the health education program?
Pages 29, 73, 86–87, 102–103, 113, 137, 161

Does it use the problem-solving approach to develop critical thinking and decision-making skills on the part of children?
Pages 48–58, 60–66, 140–154

Does it build positive mental health attitudes in children by enhancing their self-images and fostering appreciation of individual differences?
Pages 10–26, 29, 78, 86–87

---

*Based on Joint Committee on Health Problems in Education of the NEA and the AMA, *Why Health Education in Your School?* and *Suggested School Health Policies*, 5th ed., AMA.

Authors

Julius B. Richmond, M.D. Professor of Child Psychiatry and Human Development and Professor and Chairman, Department of Social and Preventive Medicine, Harvard Medical School; Director, Judge Baker Guidance Center; Chief of Psychiatric Service, Children's Hospital Medical Center, Boston, Massachusetts.

Elenore T. Pounds, M.A. Writer; lecturer; former Directing Editor of the Health and Personal Development Program; classroom teacher; coauthor of the *Health and Growth* Program; author of *Drugs and Your Safety* and other *Health Enrichment Booklets*.

Consultants

Orvis A. Harrelson, M.D., M.P.H. Corporate Medical Director, Weyerhauser Company, Tacoma, Washington; former Administrative Director of Health, Tacoma Public Schools, Tacoma, Washington.

Gladys Gardner Jenkins, M.A. Lecturer in Parent-Child-Teacher Relationships, University of Iowa, Iowa City, Iowa; former member, National Advisory Council on Child Growth and Human Development; author of *Helping Children Reach Their Potential*; coauthor of *These Are Your Children*.

Wallace Ann Wesley, Hs.D. Director, Department of Health Education, American Medical Association, Chicago, Illinois; former teacher at primary through college levels.

Learner Feedback

Experimental versions of many of the lessons in the HEALTH Program for the primary grades were used during the 1975–1976 school year with students at Levy Elementary School, Torrance, California; Mayport Elementary School, Atlantic Beach, Florida; St. Mary's School, Darien, Illinois; and Public School 276, Brooklyn, New York. The authors and editors of the program are grateful to the students and to the teachers in these schools for their comments and their suggestions.

Content Specialists

Richard H. Blum, Ph.D. Consulting Professor, Department of Psychology and Director, Joint Program in Drugs, Crime, and Community Studies, Center for Interdisciplinary Research, Stanford University, Stanford, California.

Norman H. Olsen, D.D.S. Chairman of the Department of Pedodontics and Dean of The Dental School, Northwestern University, Chicago, Illinois.

Willie D. Ford, Ph.D. Professor, Nutrition and Home Economics, Grambling State University, Grambling, Louisiana; former Nutrition Specialist, U.S. Department of Agriculture, University of Nebraska, Lincoln, Nebraska.

Marguerite Robinson, M.S. Consumer Specialist, Department of Health, Education, Welfare, Food and Drug Administration, Chicago, Illinois; Past President, Chicago Nutrition Association, Chicago, Illinois.

Lucia Guzman, B.S. Assistant to the Dean for Student Affairs, University of Texas School of Allied Health Sciences, University of Texas Medical Branch, Galveston, Texas.

Joan Tillotson, Ph.D. Consultant in Movement Education, The University of North Carolina at Charlotte, Charlotte, North Carolina.

Barbara J. Kohuth, B.S. Environmental Health Educator; Head, Office of Environmental Education and Public Information, Cleveland Department of Public Health and Welfare, Cleveland, Ohio.

Wilma Yee, B.S., R.N. Public Health Nurse and School Nurse, Oakland Public Schools, Oakland, California.

Boyd T. Marsh, M.A., Deputy Health Commissioner for Environmental Health, Cleveland Department of Public Health and Welfare, Cleveland, Ohio.

The assistance of the National Safety Council, Chicago, Illinois, in reviewing the safety advice in this material is gratefully acknowledged.

Contents

Components of Level Two

Program Materials

Pupil's Text
Centers around the special health and safety
  needs and interests of the seven- to eight-
  year-old child.
The amount of written material and the
  reading level are appropriate to second-
  grade readers.
Heavily illustrated including full color
  photographs, original art, and reproduc-
  tions of famous masterpieces.

Teacher's Edition
This *Teacher's Edition* contains the following aids:
Teacher's Supplement containing brief, professional "refresher" articles (T11-T29);
  enrichment suggestions for teaching each
  lesson (T30-T42); and reference materials
  for teachers, parents, and pupils (T43-
  T46). The complete contents are listed
  on page T6.
Instant-help "Teacher's Notes" in the upper
  margins of the pupil's pages plus answers
  to test questions.

Supplementary Materials

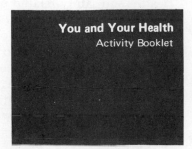

Activity Booklet
Perforated sheets in this 32-page, consumable booklet have health activities for
  school use on one side, health activities
  for *home use* and a special health message
  for parents on the other.

Features of Level Two

Chapter Openers

Each chapter begins with a distinctive introduction which conveys the meaning of the content and poses questions designed to lead the student into the chapter.

Photographic Stories

A photographic "picture story" is used to tell the children about some of the things that happen in a hospital. This story prepares children for basic hospital procedures and satisfies normal curiosity about hospitals.

Decision-Making Pages

Students are given the opportunity to make decisions about the right thing to do in the areas of safety, consumer health, and environmental health. A problem situation is shown in a full-page illustration. Students are asked what they would do in that situation. Then they are told to turn the page. When they turn the page, students find the correct thing to do in the situation shown.

Poems, Songs, and Works of Art

Health- and safety-related poems, songs, and works of art are used throughout the text. "Just Listen" pages afford the teacher an opportunity to read aloud poems that teach health and safety concepts. "Just Sing" pages provide the students with a pleasant way to learn health content through repetition. And "Just Look" pages expose the student to health-related fine art.

Health Around Us

The "Health Around Us" page appears throughout the book. It is used to make students aware of intriguing aspects of health and safety in the world around them and to highlight new developments in the field of health.

Can You Show What You Know?

This is one of several evaluative techniques used in the HEALTH Program. Here behavioral objectives in the cognitive area are posed to the students in childlike language. Students, in turn, give evidence of what they have learned by *observable behavior.*

Yes or No? and Fill in the Answer

End-of-chapter test is based on the content of the chapter. The test requires the student to give a simple yes or no answer or to complete the word to fill in a blank. End-of-book test is action-oriented.

School and Home

The "School and Home" page is the last page of each chapter in the pupil's text. This page suggests ways the child can bring home newly acquired health knowledge in order to share that knowledge with family members and to incorporate it in daily life.

Learner Feedback

YOU AND YOUR HEALTH has been developed as a result of reactions and suggestions from students and teachers who used the popular HEALTH AND GROWTH Program. Feedback from students and teachers was obtained through questionnaires, correspondence, prepublication testing, and classroom observation.

Level Two of YOU AND YOUR HEALTH contains less written material than level two of the preceding series. The reading level of the new text is on target for the grade level and an especially readable type face has been used.

The content of this text has been reorganized to emphasize cooperation between the school, the home, and the community. The opening chapter is oriented toward building positive self-images and improving students' relationships with each other and with the members of their families. The closing chapter of the text brings the student in contact with community and environmental health problems.

A "School and Home" page at the end of each chapter in YOU AND YOUR HEALTH suggests ways for the child to *bring home* the health knowledge that he or she has gained in that chapter. In addition, a new product—a *School/Home Activity Booklet*—has been made available for use with the text. This consumable booklet is designed to reinforce concepts taught in the text. Each lesson consists of an activity to be done in school, an activity to be done at home, and a health message for parents.

Other features have been included to increase student involvement and awareness of health and safety in their daily living and in the world around them. These include health poems and songs, famous works of art pertaining to some aspect of the subject matter, and articles on interesting health and safety topics.

Finally, the teachability of the Program has been enhanced. Behavioral objectives, stated in terms the students can understand, are presented as part of each chapter in YOU AND YOUR HEALTH. End-of-chapter tests are designed to test these objectives. And word lists are included in the activities for each chapter to provide vocabulary development for the student.

In order to continue Scott, Foresman's practice of making our programs responsive to the needs of students and teachers, we have included a teacher's questionnaire on pages T47 and T48. We would appreciate your completing the questionnaire and returning it to us after you have taught YOU AND YOUR HEALTH for most of the school year. If you would be willing to have your students fill out questionnaires, please let us know so that we can send you student questionnaires and return envelopes.

A Healthful Classroom Environment

If health education is to be effective, it is important that it take place in a classroom environment that is physically and mentally healthy. Here are some things you can do to create a favorable *physical environment* for children.

To create a favorable physical environment
Turn on lights on dark days and try to have chairs and desks or tables arranged so no one faces a strong light or glare.

See that children have chairs and desks that are properly adjusted to their heights.

Allow plenty of time for, and give reminders about washing hands *before* eating and *after* using the toilet.

Alternate periods of concentrated work with periods of relaxing activities; alternate periods of strenuous play with quiet ones.

See that playtimes are a mixture of undirected play and of supervised activity during which pupils may explore and practice such skills as climbing, running, and jumping.

Be aware of the needs of some children for more sleep and adequate food. Tired, hungry children do not learn.

Be alert to signs and complaints of illness—watch for change in skin color (which may indicate fever), skin eruptions, dull or watery eyes, general or unusual listleness, irritability, signs of a cold. (See "Signs and Symptoms of Illness" on page T13.)

Cooperate with others in the school system in setting up a plan for health examinations and for keeping cumulative health records.

Pay attention to the environment in general including aesthetics—as influencing the learning process.

The classroom environment which promotes mental health is one in which each child is helped to develop a strong, positive self-image; a feeling of belonging; and a sense of worth. Here are some things you can do to create such an environment.

To foster a strong, positive self-image
Make a point of learning children's names as soon as possible; check with each child to see if there is a nickname he or she prefers.

Encourage the making of self-portraits. If possible, have pupils use hand mirrors to study carefully hair color, eye color, and so on.

Post *all* the children's self-portraits in the classroom. If there isn't room, display them in "shifts" in randomly chosen order or find room in the hall outside the classroom. Be sure portraits are labeled so the child's name can be seen.

Take time for youngsters to talk about the topic "What I Like About Myself." Let them draw pictures of themselves in activities they feel they do well.

Read poems, such as the one in Chapter One, that stress each child's uniqueness.

Look for opportunities to emphasize that each youngster is different in many ways from any other human being; that he or she is "special"; that differences among individuals are natural and to be expected.

Ask children to draw pictures and write simple stories about their homes, their families, their pets, the foods they like best, things they like to do, a time when they felt sad or happy or angry.

Teach songs such as "Special" from *The Sesame Street Song Book* (Simon & Schuster).

To foster a feeling of "belonging"

Make your classroom a warm, friendly place.

Make it a point to celebrate birthdays by establishing simple ceremonies such as singing to the birthday child.

Watch out for the friendless child; do what you can to seat him or her beside outgoing youngsters and to team him or her with friendly children on committees.

When children are absent for a time, call their homes to inquire about their health. Have the class or individuals prepare simple get-well messages. Welcome back the absentees and let pupils brief them on what has happened at school during their absence.

Make special efforts to help newcomers feel comfortable. Assign friendly children to be "Big Brothers" or "Big Sisters" until the newcomers feel at home.

Let boys and girls have a part in planning various class undertakings.

Encourage the children to talk over problems that arise in the classroom and try to work out better ways of doing things.

To foster a sense of worth

Treat children as you treat your own good friends: find kindly, personal things to say; notice and comment on the positive things a child does.

Try to convey to pupils that you like them, that you have faith in them, that when something goes wrong you will try to help and to see their side of the situation.

Be friendly to *all* children and go out of your way to give an extra dose of friendliness to those who need it most—the noisy ones; the slow ones; the shy ones; the ones with problems such as divorce, illness, or unemployment in the family.

See that each child has a chance to taste success in some area—reading, singing, drawing, pantomiming, playing, caring for a classroom pet, or cleaning the chalkboard.

Build on a child's strengths, then help the child master his or her difficulties.

Keep in mind that praise for what a child has done, or tried hard to do, is a tonic that inspires greater efforts.

Evaluate a child's own progress rather than comparing him or her with others.

Help children learn to accept mistakes and to profit from them. But try to see that pupils have a variety of opportunities for successful experiences too.

Assume that a child having difficulty *wants* to learn but for some reason or other is not doing so; then try to seek the causes for the difficulty. Make use of personnel on the school staff—counselors, nurse, speech therapists, learning-disability specialists, psychologists, and so on—in seeking solutions.

Plan classroom activities to fit the abilities of each child in your room. Set goals for a child that are possible for him or her to achieve. Do not ask a child to achieve what is impossible.

Remember that the child's achievement can often be facilitated if you, the teacher, utilize all the helps at hand—supervisory bulletins, teacher's guides and resource books, courses of study, multimedia aids, an individualized curriculum, as well as sound, appealing instructional aids for pupils.

Signs and Symptoms of Illness[1]

Point of Observation	Physical Signs	Behavior	Complaint
General Appearance and Behavior	Excessive thinness or excessive overweight; very small or very large in body build for age; pallor; weary expression; fatigue; poor posture; dark circles or puffiness under eyes.	Acts tired or apathetic; is easily irritated; makes frequent trips to toilet; has persistent nervous habits, such as muscular twitching or biting of nails or lips; is subject to spasms (fits), fainting spells, or frequent nosebleeds; gets short of breath after mild exertion and climbing stairs; lacks appetite; vomits frequently.	Feels tired or is apathetic; doesn't want to play; has aches or pains; feels sick to stomach; feels dizzy.
Ears	Discharge from ear; cotton in ear; tired, strained expression long before day is over; watchful, bewildered expression.	Is persistently inattentive; asks to have questions repeated; habitually fails to respond when questioned; mispronounces common words; cocks one ear toward speaker.	Has earache; has buzzing or ringing in ears; ears feel stuffy; hears noises in head; feels dizzy.
Eyes	Inflamed (reddened) or watery eyes; frequent sties; crusted lids; cross-eye.	Holds book too close to eyes; squints at book or chalkboard; persistently rubs or blinks eyes; reads poorly.	Headache; eyes ache or smart; cannot see well (blurred vision).
Nose and Throat (Upper Respiratory Tract)	Frequent or long-continued colds; persistent nasal discharge.	Is frequently absent from school because of a cold; constantly clears throat or has frequent coughing or sneezing spells; is always sniffling or blowing nose; breathes persistently through mouth.	Throat feels sore or scratchy; has difficulty in swallowing; nose feels stuffy or sore.
Skin	Rashes or inflamed skin areas; scales and crusts; persistent sores; pimples and blackheads on face; boils; hives; persistent warts; accidental injuries, such as cuts.	Is always scratching himself; is subject to skin irritations (hives, eczema, puzzling rashes, etc.) which suggest sensitivity to one or more substances (allergic manifestations); is easily bruised.	Skin itches or burns.

[1] Courtesy of the Metropolitan Life Insurance Company.

A Developmental Profile of Seven- to Eight-Year-Olds

Health education, if it is to be effective, must be appropriate to the developmental level of the learner. The authors of YOU AND YOUR HEALTH have been aware of this need to have the health materials "on target" for the learners. Special efforts have been made to achieve this important goal.

As background for preparing a textbook geared to seven- to eight-year-olds, findings from the field of child growth and development were studied as one fertile means of learning about the particular health and safety needs, interests, and concerns of this age group. Indeed, one of the advisors on the series, Gladys Gardner Jenkins, is coauthor of a book on child growth and development for teachers and parents entitled *These Are Your Children.*[1]

Research studies about the health interests of children—such as *Teach Us What We Want to Know,*[2] a study made in Connecticut of 5,000 children's health concerns—have been utilized, as has informal research done by the authors themselves.

Furthermore, a group of experts in many health-related fields was brought together to aid in creating YOU AND YOUR HEALTH. Included in this group are two physicians, one a pediatrician and a psychiatrist and the other the director of health services in a large school district; two nutritionists; a school nurse; the head of the department of children's dentistry and dean of the dental school in a major university; a biologist; two environmentalists; an expert in child growth and development; the director of health education for the American Medical Association; a consultant in physical education; a health educator; an experienced writer for children; and *many* classroom teachers. (See the authorship group pictured on pages T4 and T5.) The combined knowledge and talents of this author-advisor-consultant group yielded a highly useful profile of seven- to eight-year-olds and their health needs. This profile was used as background for developing the textbook and related materials.

Let's have a look at the profile that has emerged from research about seven- to eight-year-olds. It is true, of course, that there is no typical child, but there *are* certain characteristics which do seem to be predominant in this age group. Some of these are described below.

Vitality and energy abound

Although Sevens are not so continually active as they were at six, they still feel the need to rush around, to do somersaults, to climb to the top of the jungle gym. They favor roller skates, jump ropes, scooters, and two-wheelers. However, Sevens show a growing ability to pace themselves by alternating strenuous and quiet play.

Sevens need a change of pace

Signs of fatigue often show during the afternoon session of school. Care needs to be taken to provide rest through a change of activity, especially during the afternoon session, and to balance active play with quieter activities. Most Sevens and Eights need about eleven hours of sleep; but sleep needs vary from child to child.

---

[1] Gladys Gardner Jenkins and Helen S. Schacter, *These Are Your Children,* 4th ed. (Scott, Foresman, 1975).
[2] Ruth Byler, Gertrude Lewis, and Ruth Totman, *Teach Us What We Want to Know* (Published for The Connecticut State Board of Education by the Mental Health Materials Center, 1969).

Restlessness may occur

Sevens are often fidgety; they find it hard to sit still and not wiggle. Their need for physical activity seems to carry over into all their behavior. They often gesture as they talk; when they read, they may shuffle their feet, move their chairs, or play with their hair. Planning a program that does not require too much sitting still will help solve this problem.

Sevens are anxious to do well

They want to learn how things are done and to do things well. Often Seven is called an "anxious" age and the "eraser" age. Sevens may erase as much as they write, so concerned are they that their work be perfect.

A sense of competition is developing

Children this age like to be "first," to get the highest grade, to paint the best picture. Many are anxious for fear their classmates will not like them.

Adult approval is sought

Sevens want the approval of both adults and children. The desire to be approved by both groups may result in conflicts, since the pattern of the adult and the pattern of the peer group are not always the same.

Children seek friendly relationships with their teacher and want to please him or her. Criticism from the teacher may make them cry or cause them to blame others for their own shortcomings.

Ethical sense is growing

Sevens are much concerned with right and wrong. They may criticize playmates who do things that do not seem desirable; they may even tattle to parents or the teacher. Some of this tattling is an attempt to win the approval of the adult. Frequently, though, it is an outlet for anxiety and concern, an attempt to reassure themselves that their own behavior is still acceptable. Sevens are seeking patterns of behavior and want to be sure they get the correct ones. They often ask, "Is it all right to do that?"

Sevens still do not have a complete sense of truthfulness or honesty or property ownership. So occasionally temptation overcomes virtue and the children may pick up little things they like—a pencil, a piece of chalk, an eraser—and slip these things into their pockets. These youngsters are more truthful than they were at six, but they are still learning.

Physical growth continues

The annual expected growth in height is two or three inches, with a gain in weight of three to six pounds.

The large muscles are still ahead of the small muscles in their development, but the child is gradually attaining greater skill in the use of the small muscles. Even so, some children show a good deal of tension when they print words, holding their pencils tightly or hunching over the paper.

Eye-hand coordination is also improving, but a considerable amount of eye rubbing is noticed among Sevens. This is a possible indication that the eyes are under some strain and that school tasks should be paced so constant eye work is not needed.

Teeth are a topic of major interest

Sevens are fascinated by the subject of teeth. This is not surprising, since there are an increasing number of gaps in their mouths as more primary teeth come out. Most children will have acquired their six-year-molars, and some will proudly show their two new "front teeth" (central incisors). Other youngsters will ask wistfully, "Why am I so slow to get my new teeth?"

Curiosity is shown about many health matters

Sevens show interest in a variety of health topics. Some health questions asked by this age group are:

"Why should you wash your hands when they look clean?"
"Why do I need sleep?"
"How can we move around and bend and twist?"
"Why do we take shots?"
"What's it like at a hospital?"
"What are germs?"
"Why should you cover sneezes?"

Interest in the body is present

Children in the primary grades want to "know all about the body" according to the Connecticut Study.[1] Young children marvel at the wonders of their bodies. They are interested in how the body grows and what enables them to move about. By second grade, there is interest in how the body looks inside.

Language has developed rapidly

Children of seven may carry on vivid conversations; they like to talk and they enjoy dramatic play.

Language is now a tool which they can use effectively in expressing disapproval. Instead of fighting, they may hurl words and walk off the scene in a huff.

Boys and girls play together in group games

Some interests are beginning to differ between the boys and the girls, perhaps due to cultural patterns. Best friends are usually of the same sex.

Accidents can be a problem

Sevens tend to be more cautious and less likely to take chances than are Sixes, but safety with dogs, safety with bicycles, and safety around fires have special pertinence for children of seven or so.

This is a good age, too, to implant in a natural way some safety precautions about medicines. Thus youngsters need to know that medicines should be taken according to directions, given only by the adult in charge, kept out of the reach of younger brothers and sisters, and so on.

---

[1] Ibid.

The Parent—Teacher Conference

A conference, for our purposes, means a face-to-face conversation between a teacher and a parent. The conference may be a part of the regularly scheduled school program or it may be called by the teacher to discuss a problem. Sometimes the parent initiates the conference because of a special concern.

Whether the goal is to become acquainted with parents, to report on how things are going in school subjects, or to work out a health problem or some other difficulty, teachers as well as parents can learn and profit from such an exchange of ideas.

A conference may last fifteen minutes or fifty. The teacher may have one or several conferences with a child's parents in the course of a school year. In any case, the pooling of information can result in a better understanding of the child and of ways in which the parents and the teacher can work together to help the youngster.

A conference calls for careful preparation. You will want to organize your thoughts in advance to be clear about what you wish to accomplish. And you may want to gather records and samples of the pupil's written work to go over with parents.

You may also want to collect information from the school nurse, the counselor, the speech therapist, and so on to have available as you explain referrals for medical or other attention.

Much that a teacher takes for granted about how children grow in the ability to share, to compromise, to take responsibility, to be self-reliant, and to be considerate of others is news to parents. You may need to explain that all children have basic emotional needs but that these needs show up in entirely different ways in different children.

What Do Parents Want to Know?

Parents want to know what and how their children are being taught. A comment such as "George is doing well" doesn't mean much to parents. More helpful is an explanation such as "George likes health. He uses some of his free time to read books about health. He reports on the books to the class, and that shows he's getting the sense of what he is reading."

Many parents want to know if there is anything they can do at home to help their child with schoolwork. You can suggest word games and number games to play at home that will augment skills without putting parents in the role of tutors.

Parents want, and should be able to get, an accurate interpretation of group-testing results given in laymen's terms. One cannot take for granted that parents know the nature of tests used.

In addition to information on academic achievement, parents often need and appreciate help on special health problems of their youngsters. Along with the school nurse, the teacher can help parents locate the community resources available for vision, speech, and hearing difficulties; dental care; immunizations; chest X rays; and emergency attention.

Ending the Conference

Close the conference on an optimistic note in order to send parents on the way with a good feeling about the conference and about their child. A minute's summary and a word about a future meeting is often useful. If that is not a sufficient signal that good-bys are in order, you can always stand up, mention that someone is waiting, and thank the parents for coming.

The "How" of Health Teaching

Effective health teaching uses a variety of learning experiences. Some techniques that have been found helpful are suggested below.

Talking Things Over

Group discussion is a valuable technique. It *does* pay to talk things over. In fact, there is research to indicate that a change in attitude can be effected as a result of *talking things over in a group situation*. In guiding group discussion:

Give children a chance to think before they talk.

Refer questions back to the children now and then; for example, "Helen, why do you think that?" or "Jim, do you agree?"

Don't call on the first child who volunteers. Wait and see if you can bring into the discussion a child who rarely volunteers.

Listen to a child's remarks and make some supporting comment about them afterwards. But always leave time for other pupils to discuss their opinions.

Once in a while inject an informal note by telling of your own experiences.

Don't hesitate to bring up important ideas the children do not think of. If possible, ask questions to bring out these ideas.

Tactfully divert the discussion from private or family information that a child may start to divulge.

Use open-ended stories to foster discussion.

Summarize the main points of the discussion and encourage the group to try out the ideas gained from the discussion.

Taking Trips

Young children gain much from such experiences as visiting a supermarket to see how perishable food is stored or a bakery to see how bread is made. Preparation for such trips should include talking over what is to be seen, what questions may be answered, and what behavior is appropriate. Follow-up activities should include a chance for sharing information.

Seeing Films and Filmstrips

Films and filmstrips are always a special treat and can be effective aids in health teaching. A carefully selected list is provided on pages T43–T46.

It is advisable to preview materials before the actual showing. This will enable you to call attention to important points or to raise questions that will be answered in the film. After the showing, give children an opportunity to discuss ideas they have gained, as well as questions they may have.

Dramatizing and Pantomiming

Youngsters love dramatizing and pantomiming, and these activities can be used profitably in connection with health and safety concepts. For example, children can act out a visit to a dentist or pretend to be a school nurse. They might also pantomime safe ways of behaving when on a school bus, what they would do if they were approached by a strange dog, safe ways to ride a bicycle, safe ways to cross a street, and so on.

Puppet shows are also popular with children. Often, in such activities as talking over one's feelings, youngsters feel more free to talk if they can speak through a puppet.

Dramatic activities and role-playing also provide a useful means of helping children plan how they will share at home the health information they are learning at school.

Enjoying Poetry

Many an important lesson is imparted joyously through a poem. What is more, children often ask to hear a favorite poem over and over. In this way the message is reinforced by repetition. Throughout the primary texts in this Program, good use is made of appropriate poems by well-known writers for children. (See pages 13, 59, 77, 89, and 110 in *Book Two*.)

Some other poems children enjoy are:

Morning Toast[1]

My toast has such a nice crunchable sound
As I bite my piece that's all buttered
  and browned.
Though my egg is pure silver and gold
  in my dish
And my orange and cocoa quite all
  one could wish
Still, I know, that at breakfast the thing
  I like most
Is my buttered, brown, munchable,
  crunchable toast!

My Nose[2]

It doesn't breathe;   I am discouraged
It doesn't smell;   With my nose:
It doesn't feel   The only thing it
So very well.   Does is blows.

Growing Up[3]

When I grow up
  (as everyone does)
What will become
  of the Me I was?

Smells[1]

The world is full of wonderful smells,
And you have a nose that always tells
Of bread in the oven, hot and nice,
Of cake being baked with lots of spice,
Of a barn with fresh-cut hay in the mows,
Of horses and pigs and cats and cows,
Of a dog when he's warm and lies in the sun,
Of applesauce and chocolate and a sugar bun.
Wouldn't it be dreadful if you'd no nose to tell
Of every wonderful, wonderful smell?

After a Bath[2]

After my bath
I try, try, try
to wipe myself
till I'm dry, dry, dry.

Hands to wipe
and fingers and toes
and two wet legs
and a shiny nose.

Just think how much
less time I'd take
if I were a dog
and could shake, shake, shake.

Since[3]

Since I MUST take a bath,
I'm glad that my nose
isn't long like the kind
that an Elephant grows,
that I haven't a neck
like a spotted Giraffe,
or an Ostrich's neck . . .
or even a HALF,
and I'm glad, as to legs,
that I only have two
instead of the number
that Centipedes do.

[1] "Morning Toast" (poem) by Doris I. Bateman from *Poems Children Enjoy*. Reprinted by permission of the author and The Instructor Publications, Inc., Dansville, New York, 14437.
[2] "My Nose" from *All Together* by Dorothy Aldis. Copyright 1925, 1926, 1927, 1928, 1934, 1939, 1952 by Dorothy Aldis. Reprinted by permission of G. P. Putnam's Sons.
[3] "Growing Up" from *Runny Days, Sunny Days* by Aileen Fisher, Abelard-Schuman, N.Y., 1958. Reprinted by permission of the author.

[1] From *Jingle Jangle* by Zhenya Gay. Copyright 1953 by Zhenya Gay. Reprinted by permission of The Viking Press, Inc.
[2] From *Up the Windy Hill* by Aileen Fisher. Published by Scott, Foresman and Company.
[3] From *Up the Windy Hill* by Aileen Fisher. Published by Scott, Foresman and Company.

Singing Health and Safety Songs

There are many songs, too, that are fun to sing, that carry a health or safety message, and that children want to sing over and over. An example of these songs can be found on page 22 of *Book Two*.

Drawing and Painting Pictures

Important health and safety ideas can be reinforced or shared with others through such activities as drawing and painting. Children can draw or paint simple pictures for health posters, for accompaniments to stories they have written, or for class or individual booklets.

Youngsters also enjoy making self-portraits and seeing their portraits displayed in the classroom or school hall.

Such activities as fingerpainting to music are fun and are also good "relaxers."

Learning by Doing

Whenever possible, children should be given a chance to put into action the health and safety ideas they are acquiring at school. For example, after the children talk about how to make a simple breakfast without any cooking—cold cereal, fruit, and milk perhaps —you might let them actually make such a breakfast at school.

After children have read about the desirability of being willing to try a food new to them, a simple tasting party at school might be held. At such a party, youngsters might have the opportunity to try small pieces of raw vegetables they may not have tasted.

When children read about a good playground game in their health text, they should be encouraged to try it the next time they go out to play.

Composing Riddles

Seven- to eight-year-olds are exceedingly fond of riddles. With a little help, they can become quite expert in making up riddles all by themselves. These riddles, in turn, can serve as good summarizers of health and safety ideas. Or the riddles can call attention to something worth featuring such as various kinds of fruits, different kinds of cereals, or various types of body movements.

Enjoying Books

The school and public libraries are wonderful sources of good children's books that convey health information in charming ways and that can be read to or by youngsters.

There are also books "to grow on," or books that deal in helpful ways with such problems as feeling left out, making friends, learning to tell truth from fancy.

Suggestions for books of "information" and books "to grow on" are provided on pages T43–T46.

Making Group Stories or Summaries

One way to summarize a group discussion is to write on the chalkboard the children's own comments. For example, here are some things a group of youngsters said as they concluded their discussion about "What is love?"

"Love is when you give your mom a hug."
"Love is when your dad takes you somewhere you always wanted to go."
"Love is when you are sick and friends send Get Well cards."
"Love is when you give your mother a present on Mother's Day."
"Love is feeling good about people."

Movement Exploration and Games

Children grow in physical well-being as they participate in vigorous muscular activity, although there are individual differences in the amount of activity required. All the body systems benefit, and endurance is improved as a result of a continuous program of guided exercise.

Boys and girls grow in self-confidence and emotional maturity, too, as they improve in fitness, gain skills, and apply these skills to such activities as games, sports, stunts, and dance. Moreover, they learn to understand and accept their own capabilities, strengths, and weaknesses, as well as those of other children.

Movement Exploration

As children explore, develop, and use basic movements, they discover the many ways they can move their bodies. A good way to approach the teaching of movement exploration is through a problem-solving method. With this method, pupils are encouraged to move in any way they wish in an attempt to solve a given problem. Some problems for primary pupils are suggested here.

Nonlocomotor Movement Exploration

Nonlocomotor movements are movements in which the body moves in and through space, but "in place," without traversing distance; the movements can be to and fro, high and low, wide and narrow, big and small.

Children can experiment with bending, stretching, kicking in place, and twisting. To be sure they understand the basic movements they are performing, children should be asked to explain what they have discovered and to observe others who perform the task in different ways.

After children have explored initial movement possibilities, you may direct further exploration by asking such questions as, "What can you do with your head? Your arms? Your feet?" Responses to these specific problems will still be individual in nature but will be focused on a central theme to which *all* children can react.

Pupils can also explore movement from a *sitting* position. They may sit on the floor and move in as many ways as possible in this position. Bending, twisting, and stretching will be experienced and should be encouraged. When children have exhausted their own exploratory movements, you can suggest further exploration with such questions as "How tall can you be?" or "How small can you be?" Then let pupils combine the movements by starting off being small and then gradually growing tall and vice versa.

Locomotor Movement Exploration

Locomotor movements, or movements which get them places, are greatly enjoyed by youngsters. A variety of locomotor movements can be explored and identified by pupils. You can ask children in small groups to move from one place on the floor to another place in any way they wish, guarding against collision with others. Again children should be asked to tell how they moved (walked, ran, skipped, galloped, hopped, jumped).

Children rarely need images to stimulate locomotor movements because they are naturally active and enjoy experimenting with ways of going about in space. However, they do enjoy and benefit from carrying out such suggestions as imitating the way different animals move.

Games

Following are examples of games that are appropriate for seven- to eight-year-olds.

Circle Stride Ball

Players form a circle with feet spread about one foot apart and touching the feet of players on either side of them. *It* stands in the circle and attempts to throw the playground ball or volleyball out of the circle between the outspread legs of the players. The players may stop the ball only with their hands and may not bend their knees or squat. A player who lets the ball out of the circle becomes the new *It*.

Shadow Tag

An *It* is chosen and attempts to tag another player by stepping on his or her shadow. Considerable skill can be developed by trying to manipulate the shadow so *It* cannot step on it. Bending, twisting, and stooping can cause the shadow to shift so touching it is difficult. A player may also escape being tagged by running to the shade.

Note: Bending, twisting, stopping, and starting make excellent movement patterns for exploration before moving into this game. Immediate reinforcement of movement problems by use of a game situation is sound teaching.

Move and Freeze

Have children scatter around the room. Ask them to move any way they wish as you clap your hands, then FREEZE when you stop clapping. *You* may direct specific movements such as skipping and freezing, hopping and freezing, and so on, although it is better to have the movement ideas come from the children. Encourage listening skills and creative ideas for freezing in different positions, with the emphasis on a controlled balance rather than on a silly, uncontrolled shape.

Creative Dance

Creative dance is a fine medium for expressing the self. Through creative dance one can act out, communicate, and share ideas and emotions. Basic nonlocomotor movements such as *bending*, *twisting*, and *stretching*, as well as such locomotor movements as *walking*, *running*, *skipping*, *sliding*, and *galloping*, should be continued throughout the lower elementary grades. Children can move to the accompaniment of piano, percussion instruments, or recordings.

Children's movements may vary in *level* or in *direction*. Thus children may bend high or low or stretch up or out. Children may walk on tiptoes or with their knees bent. They may skip forward or backward, in circles or in squares.

Seven- to eight-year-olds can begin to practice these movements with a partner. With inside hands joined, children can walk together, skip together, run together. Thus they learn to synchronize their movements both with the accompaniment and with the movements of another child.

When this is accomplished, a child and his or her partner can walk, run, and skip in small circles. Partners should join both hands and move first around to the left, then at the change of the musical phrase move to the right. Partners can also move side by side, with inside hands joined. They can run, skip, and gallop forward together.

Playground Activities and Safety

Active children have a desire and a need to climb, swing, hang, and turn upside down. Playground equipment can provide an effective means for such activities, but supervision is needed to be sure of its safe use.

Talking with children about such safety guides as the following is important as you teach the correct use of apparatus:

When jumping to the ground from a piece of equipment, be sure to bend your knees as you land.

Do not interfere with, or distract, a child who is on the apparatus.

Never play on apparatus if it is wet or slippery due to rain or snow.

Know what you can and cannot do on each piece of apparatus. If you want to try something new, ask the teacher to help you. (Although children are naturally cautious and rarely try activities beyond their abilities, they may be "dared" or chided into unsafe action.)

The apparatus activities that follow can be taught to second-graders.

Swings: Children can learn how to swing while sitting down and how to stop the swing safely to get off. Children should be reminded to stop any swing which is moving with no one on it. Tell them to hold on with both hands while swinging. Remind them only one person at a time is allowed on a swing, and they should never stand while swinging.

Jungle Gym and *Rainbow Climber:* Children can crawl under, around, and between the rungs. They can learn to climb to safe heights and return to the ground.

Horizontal Ladder: A child should not be allowed on a horizontal ladder unless able to reach it without assistance. The child should not be lifted up or be allowed to use a box to reach equipment. On the horizontal ladder, children can learn to hang by their hands, swing their bodies to and fro as they hang, and drop safely to the ground landing on their feet with their knees slightly bent.

At this age children can begin to learn how to travel across the ladder. They should first be taught the *side travel*. In this activity, they hold tightly with both hands on one side rail. They inch along the side rail from one end of the ladder to the other.

Physical Education References
Movement Exploration and Games
Anderson, Marian H., et al. *Play with a Purpose: Elementary School Physical Education.* 2d ed. Harper, 1972.

Association for Childhood Education International. *Physical Education for Children's Healthful Living.* ACEI, 1968.

Barlin, Anne, and Barlin, Paul. *The Art of Learning Through Movement.* Ward Ritchie, 1971.

Carr, Rachel E. *Be a Frog, a Bird, or a Tree: Creative Yoga Exercises for Children.* Doubleday, 1973.

Dauer, Victor P. *Dynamic Physical Education for Elementary School Children.* 5th ed. Burgess, 1975.

Fabricius, Helen. *Physical Education for the Classroom Teacher.* 2d ed. W. C. Brown, 1972.

Hackett, Layne C., and Jenson, Robert G. *A Guide to Movement Exploration.* Peek Publications, 1967.

Porter, Lorena. *Movement Education for Children: A New Direction in Elementary School Physical Education.* NEA, 1969.

Witkin, Kate and Philp, Richard. *To Move, to Learn.* Temple University Press, 1977. Also available in paperback.

Creative Dance
Ashton, Dudley. *Rhythmic Activities: Grades K-6.* AAHPER, 1964.

Clark, Carol E. *Rhythmic Activities for the Classroom.* Instructor, 1969.

Dimondstein, Geraldine. *Children Dance in the Classroom.* Macmillan, 1971.

La Salle, Dorothy. *Rhythms and Dances for Elementary Schools.* Rev. ed. Ronald, 1951.

Murray, Ruth L. *Dance in Elementary Education.* 2d ed. Harper, 1963.

Pounds, Elenore T., and Tillotson, Joan S. *Moving, Moving, Moving About.* Scott, Foresman, 1973.

Sheehy, Emma D. *Children Discover Music and Dance.* Teachers College Press, 1968.

Films and Filmstrips for the Teacher
Series of twenty-four cartridged film-loops: *Basic Movement* (6 loops); *Movement Awareness* (5 loops); *Basic Manipulative Activities* (7 loops); *Functional Fitness* (6 loops) (Ealing Films).

Introduction to Body Movements: Locomotor Skills (Silver Burdett).

Learning Through Movement (S-L Productions).

Series of four films: *Movement Education: Guided Exploration; Movement Education in Physical Education; Movement Education: The Problem-Solving Technique; Movement Education: Time and Space Awareness* (University of Iowa).

A Time to Move (Early Childhood Productions).

Family-Life Education

Many teachers and parents who are competent and understanding in other areas find themselves having difficulty with sex education. It may help many of them relax if they realize that answering questions and teaching the facts about procreation constitute a very small part of this education.

Sex education is not accomplished solely by teaching facts. Youngsters develop attitudes toward their own bodies, feelings about themselves as boys or girls, and acceptance of their responsibilities toward other family members and toward those outside the family by absorbing the attitudes of the adults with whom they come in contact. Parents' expression of love and respect for one another and for their children is good education in sexuality.

Children are also influenced by what they learn from books, newspapers, comics, and television; from advertisements that stress false aspects of sexual attraction; and from information or misinformation from their friends. Youngsters learn from stories, comments, and practices that emphasize stereotyped sex roles, with the all-too-frequent downgrading of the abilities and achievements of women. Such downgrading warps the concepts of both girls and boys as they learn to accept or reject their biological sex.

Youngsters are quick to realize whether boys or girls are more valued in the home, or if there are subtle differences in expectations or attitudes toward boys and girls in their classrooms or school programs.

It is important that the significant adults in children's lives take time to help them clarify the information they have obtained so that children have true rather than distorted facts. Adults also need to help

children at this formative period to develop healthy attitudes toward sex and the part it will play in their lives.

We can see how important it is for us as teachers to have an understanding of how the sexual drive develops and the part it plays in life—and to be able to accept it as a normal, healthy, integral part of our lives. With such an understanding we can help foster wholesome attitudes in the children we teach, particularly in reinforcing concepts of the importance of the family.

However, it is essential to be aware that the children we teach come from many different kinds of families. We should avoid stereotyping the family as the nuclear family or as one in which father always works and mother always stays home. Some children live in one-parent homes; others live in foster homes or with relatives. Many children will have complicated family relationships as a result of their parents' remarriages. If we do not avoid stereotyping, many children will be hurt and perhaps look upon their own family arrangement as somehow not a real family—when, in truth, their homes, diverse as they may be, may be giving the supporting, loving care which makes a family.

Children need to understand, accept, and be prepared for the parental role. Thus, another part of sex education is helping youngsters—even in the primary years—begin to understand the value of family life as a framework for developing human relationships and responsibilities and for learning how to love and be loved.

Family-Life Education at School

Ideally the biological side of sex education should be given at home from the time the child asks questions about how babies are born. The part that the home plays in teaching the child about life and how it begins is indeed important.

The Scott, Foresman HEALTH Program offers a variety of aids to schools. In the pupils' texts of this Program at the primary levels, strong and persistent efforts are made to foster communication between each child and the family. At the end of each chapter, there is a section entitled "School and Home." Here children are encouraged to talk over with the family the health and safety ideas they are learning at school; to share in the work of the family; and to talk over their problems, questions, or feelings. With communication channels kept open, children may feel more free to ask questions about birth and reproduction too.

Also in this Program, much emphasis is put on developing warm human relationships. Thus primary-age youngsters are led to think about what we mean by *love* and about ways of expressing love. For example, pupils act out ways of showing love for others. In the same way, youngsters later explore *kindness* and ways of showing it. The idea that all human beings have feelings is also emphasized. Ways of coping with feelings such as anger and fear are considered as well. Such very human approaches and emphases offer a background against which more specific sex education instruction can be given.

Teacher-Parent Cooperation

Some parents who feel inadequate to give their children needed information will turn to the school and to the teacher for help and advice. The well-informed teacher can do much to cooperate with parents, both through individual conferences and through well-planned open house or PTA meetings.

A teacher can also make material available to parents who seek help. Point out that when children ask questions, they ought to be given honest answers. Since children ask questions from a childlike frame of reference, answers should be simple and direct, giving only information requested. The material[1] below suggests answers to some commonly asked questions of primary-age children.

Why are girls' bodies different from boys'?
Emphasize that boys and girls are *born* to be different. Only women can give birth to babies, and only men can be fathers. The special place where a baby grows inside the mother's body *(uterus)* is found only in women; there is no such place in men's bodies.

A man's role is to help start the baby in the mother's body and later to help care for the children.
How does a baby get inside the mother?
In special places in the mother's body, the *ovaries*, there are many tiny cells called *egg cells*. When one of the egg cells inside the mother is joined by a *sperm cell* from the father's body, the growth of a baby is started. If the child wants to know more, you can explain that the sperm cells are contained in a fluid called *semen* that comes from the father's body. A word of caution needs to be given about a commonly used description of the father's role as that of "planting a seed" to start the baby. This description can give a child some strange notions. Some children may think of "seeds"

[1] Adapted by permission from *Parents' Guide to Facts of Life for Children.* Child Study Association of America/Wel-Met Inc. © 1965 by Maco Magazine Corporation.

in connection with swallowing fruit pits, and assume, as many primitive people have, that birth is part of the digestive process.

How does the mother know when the baby is ready to be born?

The special place where the baby grows in the mother's body has powerful muscles in it. When it is time for the baby to be born, these muscles start to work hard with a steady rhythm to push the baby out into the world. When the mother feels the muscles working, she knows that the baby is on its way to being born.

How does the baby get out of the mother's body at birth?

The mother's muscles push the baby through a special passageway called the *vagina*. This passageway gets wider, like a rubber band being stretched, to allow the baby to move through. The baby comes out between the mother's legs.

Does it hurt to have a baby?

The action of the powerful muscles that push the baby out of the mother's body does cause the mother some discomfort, but the woman's body is made so that it can manage the birth process successfully.

Reading Lists

Parents often appreciate knowing about books or booklets that can help them clarify concepts of family life to their children. From these materials parents can gain ease and familiarity in phrasing the ideas they want to talk over with their children. Often a book prepared for children can be read aloud by a parent, with the information in the book serving as a springboard to discussion. Most of the following materials are available at local libraries.

For Children

Brenner, Barbara. *Bodies*. Dutton, 1973. Fine photographs of what a body is made of, how it differs from other things, how it works.

De Schweinitz, Karl. *Growing Up: How We Become Alive, Are Born, and Grow*. Rev. ed. Macmillan, 1965. Simple enough for an eight-year-old to read.

Gruenberg, Sidonie M. *The Wonderful Story of How You Were Born*. Rev. ed. Doubleday, 1970. Although written for children, this book contains a Guide for Parents.

Pounds, Elenore T. and Fricke, Irma. *Beginning the Human Story: A New Baby in the Family*. Scott, Foresman, 1977. Paperback. Includes notes for the teacher to help answer questions.

Shapp, Martha; Shapp, Charles; and Shepard, Sylvia. *Let's Find Out About Babies*. Watts, 1975. Includes human and animal babies.

Showers, Paul. *A Baby Starts to Grow*. T. Y. Crowell, 1969. Simply written so that young children can read it themselves, this book describes how a baby grows before becoming strong enough to live outside the mother's body.

For Parents and Teachers

Child Study Association. *What to Tell Your Child About Sex*. Pocket Books, 1974. Paperback.

Lerrigo, Marion O., and Southard, Helen. *Parents' Responsibility*. Medical consultant, Milton J. E. Senn. Rev. ed. AMA and NEA, 1970.

If Children Ask About Death[1]

By Gladys Gardner Jenkins

Children are curious about the beginnings of life. They are also curious about death. As teachers, we may be called upon to answer children's questions about death, to comfort a bereaved child, or on rare occasion to tell of the death of a classmate. At such times, we need to remember that the child's capacity to understand death will depend upon cognitive development plus experience.

One factor involved in understanding death is the cognitive knowledge of the facts of death as the end of life in the body. These facts can be given by a sensitive teacher as a child comes upon death—the flowers that die, the dead bird found on a walk, the death of a classroom gerbil. Later, as children gradually come to understand and appreciate the life cycle as it affects all living things, death will be put in perspective.

But understanding death also involves deep feelings. By the careful choice of stories children can be drawn into some of the feelings and concerns we all have about the death of a person for whom we care. Children have responded for many years to E. B. White's book *Charlotte's Web* (Harper).

However, some books today are presented with such realism that they may precipitate anxiety in children instead of developing understanding. For instance, a realistic presentation of the death of a grandparent may arouse anxiety in a child who had never thought of the death of a loved grandparent as imminent. A picture of the end of all living things might be a forceful lesson in ecology but a devastating thought for a young child.

[1] This article has been added to the *Teacher's Supplement* at the request of many teachers who have used previously published health materials by Scott, Foresman and Company.

Learning to accept reality is important. But the readiness of a child to be faced with reality which does not come from experience must be carefully weighed. It may be harmful rather than useful to stimulate imagination and provoke thoughts before the child has the resources to cope with them.

It is difficult to know what children are actually feeling, what their concerns, interpretations, and thoughts about death may be. This is why it is important to provide an atmosphere in the classroom in which children will feel free to ask questions and share ideas if the subject of death occurs.

Teachers may also be called upon to help children in their classrooms when the experience of death touches them through the loss of a parent, grandparent, sibling, friend, or classmate. This occasion may also call for facts, but the facts will now be interspersed with deep emotional feelings.

Death of one who has been close becomes a painful separation. Some children feel angry: "Why did my father leave me?" Many children, and many adults, have a feeling of guilt: "What did I do?" This feeling can be very strong and add anxiety to the grief of separation. A child should be reassured by being told the real cause of the death. There is also a fear that others whom the child loves may die, leaving the child with no one to care for him or her. Again, reassurance is needed.

Many children cannot express these feelings in words but show them in behavior. A child may become more demanding of attention or may cling to an adult. Older children may be so full of their thoughts that they can no longer focus on their schoolwork. Some children may not want to play with their friends or take part in activities which they previously had enjoyed. Others cover their feelings by being aggressive or by acting as if nothing had happened. These are clues that the children need our help.

Grief in a child must have an outlet. The child who seems so brave, who does not cry, who goes about life as usual may be bottling up a deep grief that may cause difficulty at a later time. It does not help children to tell them to be brave, not to cry, to be a big boy or girl. Children need to grieve for a time. Neither does it help for adults to hide their grief, although hysterical grief can be deeply disturbing to children.

It is not wise to arouse thoughts of extra responsibilities such as: "You will be the man of the house" or "You will be the little mother now." Neither is it helpful to use the memory of the person who has died to encourage effort or better behavior. These are burdens a child is not able to carry. Such suggestions only build anxiety. In addition, it is better to talk about memories of a real person rather than a glorified one.

The most helpful support we can give as teachers is to let the child know that we do understand the mixed-up feelings, that we are ready to listen if talk would help, and that we will answer questions as honestly as we can. Often, too, the physical comfort of an arm around the child, or a shoulder on which to cry, can bring great relief.

If a child in the class dies, the other children will be tense and anxious. They can more easily accept death for old people than for another child whom they have known. The death of a classmate may arouse fear of death for oneself. The children should be told the truth about their classmate's death. It is wise to help them talk about it and to help them share their feelings and concerns. Discuss what they would like to remember about their classmate and what could be done as a special remembrance.

Such an open discussion may lead to questions about death. Some children may want to talk about the funeral, about burial, or about cremation. It can be explained that different groups of people have different customs or their own special ways of saying good-by. The most difficult questions to answer will be those that might be raised about life after death. The children will come from homes of many religious faiths. What they have been taught at home will influence what they believe to be true. Each religious faith explains what happens according to its own beliefs. A teacher should neither contradict the religious teaching of the home nor express his or her own religious beliefs.

Here are some books that can help a teacher meet situations involving death.

Harris, Audrey. *Why Did He Die?* Lerner, 1971.

Kübler-Ross, Elisabeth. *Questions and Answers on Death and Dying.* Macmillan, 1974.

LeShan, Eda. *Learning to Say Good-by: When a Parent Dies.* Macmillan, 1976. Also available in paperback.

Mitchell, Marjorie Editha. *The Child's Attitude to Death.* Schocken, 1967.

Stein, Sara Bonnett. *About Dying.* Walker, 1974.

Zolotow, Charlotte. *My Grandson Lew.* Harper, 1974. (A book for children)

Enrichment Suggestions for Chapter 1
About You[1]

Overview

Chapter One focuses on mental health. It offers deeply human approaches designed to enhance self-concepts, to stress the universality of human emotions, to demonstrate ways of showing kindness and consideration for others, and to help children cope with mistakes in a mentally healthy manner.

The chapter is *activity oriented.* Boys and girls draw self-portraits, listen to a poem, discuss various kinds of feelings, explore how emotions can be expressed in body movements, act out ways to show kindness, sing a song about "Everyone Makes Mistakes," and enjoy a work of art. Such material is well adapted to lively, active children.

Important Ideas Developed in the Chapter

Each person is special; each is unique.
All people have emotions, or feelings.
Everyone's feelings change from time to time.
Some common human emotions are those of joy, sadness, pride, worry, loneliness, and anger.
Kindness involves being friendly, considerate, and thoughtful to others.
Everyone makes mistakes.
You can learn from your mistakes and then may not make the same ones again.
When you are worried or upset, it often helps to talk things over with parents or some other grown-up.

Behavioral Objectives

See page 27 in the pupil's book where behavioral objectives in the cognitive area are posed directly to pupils in simple, childlike terms. See also some hoped-for objectives,

[1] See page T43 for Reference Materials related to this chapter.

mainly in the affective area, set forth in the "Teacher's Notes" for page 27.

8–9 *About You* (Chapter-Opening Pages)

Use the questions on page 9 to start off preliminary discussion. Give help with the word *special.*

Youngsters might start a collection of pictures for a bulletin-board display. Pictures of people from newspapers or magazines whose faces express various emotions could be displayed under a caption such as WE ALL HAVE FEELINGS.

10–11 *Are You Just Like Anyone Else?*

Volunteers might line up in front of the classroom as living examples of how each individual is unique.

Point out that people not only *look* different but act and do things differently. People differ in things they can do well and things they cannot do so well, things they like to do and things they do not like to do, size and make-up of their families, and the kind of place they live.

12–13 *Just Listen*

Your pupils may want to make an "Art Gallery" featuring *their* self-portraits. These portraits can be displayed on the bulletin board or in a special class book.

You might have the poem read in verse-choir fashion, with *all* reading the first four lines. Then various individuals read the sentences about walking, talking, playing, and saying; and *all* join in again on the ending, "I am special. I am me. There's no one I'd rather be than me!"

Students might want to write a class verse (with the teacher at the board as they put it together) about being one's self and different from all others.

14–15 *How Are You Like Others?*

Youngsters might enjoy playing the game "Oh, Henry" or "Oh, Mary." Using either of these phrases, various children say it in different tones. Others guess whether the feeling of joy, anger, surprise, or fear is being expressed. This activity increases children's awareness of voice as an indication of a person's feelings.

16–17 *How Do You Feel at School?*

Use the information on this page to underscore the idea that our feelings shift. Thus, on a given day a child may feel proud at school about something he or she has done, surprised about something that has happened, a little worried about something not understood fully, and so on. Be sure children understand that adults' feelings change too.

Such sentence-starters as the following can be used for discussion. Or boys and girls might write a sentence or two and draw a picture to go with their writing.

"Once I felt happy at school when . . ." or "Once I felt unhappy at school when . . ." or "Once I felt proud at school when . . ."

Be sure that pupils know examples don't have to be limited to grades they have received. Let them know that such examples as getting along with people, helping others, being good citizens, and being good friends can be included.

This would also be a good time for you to share with your class the things that make you happy or unhappy or proud.

18–19 *How Do You Show Kindness?*

A perceptive book you might get at the library and read to your pupils is *He's My Brother* by Joe Lasker (A. Whitman). It is the story of how a family reaches out with kindness to Jamie, who is "different."

This is a good time, too, to make plans for showing kindness when someone in the group is home sick for a while. Plans may include sending get-well messages or writing "just for fun" stories to entertain the sick youngster.

20–21 *How Does It Feel to Make Mistakes?*

Expand the discussion on mistakes by asking, "How often would it happen that all pupils in a group would make the same mistakes?" (Not very often. Everyone is different; we all do some things well and other things not so well.)

Emphasize that mistakes are to be expected now and then, and that it is better to be willing to try unfamiliar things and to make mistakes than to be afraid of trying new experiences for fear of making mistakes or doing poorly.

You might also have boys and girls write a sentence or two to complete this sentence-starter: "Once I made a mistake when . . ." They might draw pictures to accompany their stories.

22 *Just Sing*

Children might also sing songs they think are happy ones.

23 *Just Look*

Explore with youngsters some of the various ways by which we express feelings. Thus, artists express feelings through pictures they draw or paint or through statues they create; musicians express feelings through the music they play or create. Children can express feelings, too, in drawing, painting, music, acting, and other art forms.

24 *Health Around Us*

Ask youngsters about things they often *hear* that make them feel happy. Some examples are an oral invitation "Can you come over to play?" or a compliment "I like your new sweater."

25–26 *Things to Do* and *More Things to Do*

Youngsters might also jump rope to such rhythmic chants as "k - i - n - d spells *kind*," with one skip to each letter and one for the word.

Boys and girls might enjoy making lists of words that tell "How I feel when I am angry"; for example, *mad, ugly, mean, loud, sassy, rude, hateful, bad.* Discuss, too, how angry feelings can be changed to more pleasant ones. (By talking things over with an adult, for instance.)

27 *Can You Show What You Know?*

To help children further apply what they have been learning, have them tell or act out what they would do in a situation like this: "A little girl on the playground is crying. She has lost a nickel. What could *you* do to help?"

28 *Yes or No?*

You might do the following for another informal test. Say a word and invite pupils to tell all the things the word suggests. Some words you might use are these: *kindness, feelings, mistakes.*

29 *School and Home*

Some other ways in which parents can be informed about health ideas that are being taught at school and in which teachers can learn of special health concerns of parents are listed below.

Sending the health text home

At some convenient time, the health text might be sent home with pupils. An accompanying note might invite parents to scan the text to see what health ideas are being presented at school. Their comments might also be encouraged.

Giving parents a brief overview of the text

Since there is no area of the curriculum in which parents' active cooperation is needed more, a special attempt might be made at a room meeting of parents to give them a brief run-through of the content in the health text. You might even read aloud a selection or so. Parents are often pleased and surprised to learn how their teachings at home are being enriched and reinforced at school.

Using the *Activity Booklet*

Special messages about pertinent health topics being taught at school are included for parents on the "Home" side of each sheet in the *Activity Booklet*. (See page T7.)

Enrichment Suggestions for Chapter 2
About Your Senses and Your Safety[1]

Overview

Chapter Two centers around the five main senses, how they keep us in touch with the world around us, and most especially how the senses and the brain help keep us safe.

A problem-solving approach is used in connection with lessons on safety with dogs, safety with fire, and safety with bicycles, as well as safety with medicines and safety on school trips. Everyday problem situations are posed in text and pictures; youngsters make tentative decisions about how to solve them, and check their ideas with the correct safety solutions. Positive teaching is stressed. Children never see unsafe actions pictured in the safety treatments.

Important Ideas Developed in the Chapter

The five main senses are those of seeing, hearing, touching, smelling, and tasting.

Messages are carried over nerves from the sense organs to the brain and you decide what to do about the messages.

The most important person in keeping you safe is YOU.

Stand still and talk quietly to a dog that is menacing, then walk slowly past it.

Avoid teasing a dog; leave pets alone when they are eating or sleeping.

Try not to excite a dog by playing rough games with it.

Bicycle riders should know and use the correct hand signals for turns.

Ride one on a bicycle; ride single file; have a light, a horn, and a carrier (if needed) on your bicycle.

Walk a bicycle across a busy street.

If your clothes catch on fire, roll on the

[1] See page T44 for Reference Materials related to this chapter.

ground or try to smother the fire with a coat.

Never play with matches. Light matches or a stove only when a grown-up is with you.

Lighted matches or cigarettes thrown carelessly can start forest fires.

Never take another person's medicine.

Medicine should be given by grown-ups.

Never take a strange pill.

Medicines should be kept out of reach of little children.

Use medicines according to directions.

On a bus, stay in your seat and do not put your head or arms out the window; keep in line while getting on and off a bus.

On trips stay with the group at all times; do not touch machines in places you visit.

There are many safety helpers and safety signs in the world around you.

Behavioral Objectives

See page 70 in the pupil's book where behavioral objectives in the cognitive area are posed directly to pupils.

See also some hoped-for objectives, mainly in the affective area, set forth in the "Teacher's Notes" for page 70.

30–31 *About Your Senses and Your Safety* (Chapter-Opening Pages)

Use the questions to serve as motivators for reading the chapter and to explore children's ideas about their safety needs.

32–33 *How Do You Know What Goes On Around You?*

You might check out from the school or public library some simple reference books on the senses. A very easy book is *My Five Senses* by Aliki (T. Y. Crowell).

34-35 *How Do Your Eyes Help?*

See if children can figure out how the eyeballs are protected. Have them feel around the eyes for clues. (The eyes are protected by the bones of the cheeks and forehead.)

Ask, "What ways can *you* think of in which your eyes help keep you safe?" (You can see people and not bump into them and you can see things and not trip over them.)

36-37 *How Do Your Ears Help?*

Ask, "What have you learned about your ears that you did not know before?" (Pupils may have thought the outer ears were all there was to the ears! They may comment on the parts of the ear we cannot see.) You might explain that the outer ear helps direct sounds into the middle and inner ear.

38-39 *How Does Your Nose Help?*

See if pupils can tell of a time when the sense of smell helped them or their family members note signs of potential danger.

40-41 *How Does Your Tongue Help?*

Explain that, as the picture indicates, we taste sweet things mostly on the tip of the tongue, salty and sour things mostly on the sides of the tongue, and bitter things mostly at the back of the tongue.

The senses of *taste* and *smell* "go together." So when we have a cold or a stuffy nose, we cannot taste our food because we often cannot smell it as we usually do.

42-43 *How Do Your Fingers Help?*

Ask, "What would happen if you did not have a sense of touch?" (You would touch hot things and get burned because you would not feel the heat, and so on.)

Children might start a collection of things that are interesting and safe to touch—pieces of fur, satin, sandpaper, tree bark, and so on.

You might want to point out that we usually use more than one sense at a time. For instance, we may *see* an orange, *smell* it, and *taste* it. We may *touch* it as we peel it, and *hear* it squish as we chew it.

44-45 *What Does Your Brain Do?*

Mention that we can think very rapidly with the brain. For example, we may hear the alarm go off in the morning. The ears send the sound message to the brain. We think about the message and then send a message to the muscles. Next, the muscles move and we get out of bed—all in a very short period of time.

46-47 *How Do Messages Get to Your Brain?*

Explain that we do not always send orders for action when messages come to the brain. Sometimes we just think about the messages, as when a picture is seen on the wall. Sometimes we just enjoy the messages, as when lovely music is played.

48-51 *How Would You Act with a Strange Dog?*

Youngsters might draw safety pictures about pet safety and put them in the class book, *Keeping Safe.*

52-55 *What Should a Bicycle Driver Know?*

The number of bicycle-associated accidents begins to rise among children age seven or so; by the age of eight, bicycle-connected accidents are nearly as high as in the peak years of ten to thirteen.

Another bicycle-safety precaution is to avoid show-off stunts such as taking your hands off the handlebars.

56–58 *What If Your Clothes Catch on Fire?*
Discuss how to report a fire *at home*. GET OUT OF THE HOUSE AT ONCE AND CALL FROM A NEIGHBOR'S PHONE: Dial 0 for Operator, give the address of the fire and your name.

Stress that it is always more desirable to have an adult report the fire. But children should know how to do so if necessary. Let children act out how to report a fire.

59 *Just Listen*
Talk over how the family can put out a campfire safely. (By smothering it with some earth; by sprinkling water on it.)

60–63 *Should You Take Another Person's Medicine?*
Drug education for primary-age children generally centers around safety factors.

Discuss with pupils the special tops that are now used on medicine bottles—tops designed to keep young children from being able to open the bottles.

64–66 *How Can You Be Safe on a Class Trip?*
To emphasize safe ways of riding on school buses, chairs might be arranged to resemble the seats on a bus. Pupils can act out various ways of boarding, riding, and getting off the bus.

67 *Safety Around Us*
Youngsters might take a safety walk with you around the neighborhood of the school.

The purpose would be to find safety signs and other safety aids.

68 *Things to Do*
Children might make simple safety posters about bicycle safety.

Review with the group any accidents that have occurred in the classroom, in the school hall, or on the playground lately. Ask, "What *caused* the accident? How could it have been prevented?"

69 *Do You Remember?*
Another safety aspect to review with children is how to prevent *falls*. Falls are common among primary-age children. Often falls result from running around without looking where one is going, from unsafe play on playground equipment, and from climbing on places where one should not be climbing. The need to wipe up spilled liquids at once should also be reviewed.

70 *Can You Show What You Know?*
Put the pictures children draw about keeping safe into the class book on that topic.

71–72 *Yes or No?* and *Fill in the Answer*
For an informal checkup, say a word such as *bicycle* and invite children to tell all the safety ideas the word suggests.

For another informal checkup, ask children to write a sentence or two about something they learned in this chapter that they did not know before.

73 *School and Home*
This page works well in conjunction with the *Activity Booklet* that is available for use with this health text. (See page T7.)

Enrichment Suggestions for Chapter 3
About Your Health Questions[1]

Overview

Chapter Three centers around health questions often asked by youngsters of seven to eight or so. The questions fall mainly in the areas of The Human Body: Growth and Development; and Personal Health, Fitness, and Dental Health.

Important Ideas Developed in the Chapter

Each child is different; each has his or her own way of growing.

If children get enough of the right food, sleep, and exercise, they will grow in the way that is right for them.

We need different kinds of food each day.

We need foods each day from the four food groups: Milk Group, Fruits and Vegetables Group, Meat Group, and Breads and Cereals Group.

Different families may have widely differing food preferences and patterns of eating.

Sleep gives us energy for work and play.

When we haven't had enough sleep, we may be tired and cross and more prone to make mistakes.

Children of seven or so need about eleven hours of sleep at night, although sleep needs vary somewhat.

Exercise helps us keep healthy, helps build strong muscles, and can be fun.

We can bend and twist and turn because of our skeletal structure; the skeleton has bending places called joints.

By washing our hands before eating or handling food and after using the toilet, we help wash away germs.

A doctor conducts health checkups and gives shots to help keep us in good health.

Teeth should be brushed after meals, if possible; otherwise, they should be brushed thoroughly at least once a day.

Flossing helps clean between the teeth.

Permanent teeth are growing in the jaws under the primary teeth.

A pharmacist is a health worker; he or she fills a doctor's prescription for medicine.

Behavioral Objectives

See page 111 in the pupil's book where behavioral objectives in the cognitive area are posed directly to pupils.

See also some hoped-for objectives, mainly in the affective area, set forth in the "Teacher's Notes" for page 111.

74-75 *About Your Health Questions* (Chapter-Opening Pages)

Use questions on this page to get at what is on your pupils' minds in regard to health matters. Jot down queries as they are raised. If the questions are not answered in the chapter, pupils could use simple reference books or talk to the school nurse.

76-77 *How Will You Find Answers to Health Questions?* and *Just Listen*

In addition to the sources shown on these pages, pupils may mention the *doctor*. The doctor can be asked questions during health checkups.

78 *Why Aren't Children the Same Age the Same Size?*

Comment, "There are other ways to grow besides growing taller and heavier. What do you think some of those ways are?" (We can grow in ability to get along with others, to read better, to play ball, and so on.)

---

[1] See page T44 for Reference Materials related to this chapter.

79-85 *What Kinds of Foods Should You Eat?*

Youngsters might make up riddles about foods for the others to guess. For example: It is round. It is red. It is good in salads. Its name starts with *t*. What is it?

In the discussion, make it clear that the four food groups are a suggested daily guide, and that it is desirable to follow it most of the time. But there will be days when the food guide is not followed exactly. Point out that we need water in the daily diet too.

86-87 *Do Different Families Eat Different Foods?*

Youngsters might tell what they think is their family's best-liked food. List the various suggestions on the chalkboard. Use the list as an example of the fact that different families have different food preferences. Point out that "different" does not mean better or worse—just *different*.

88-89 *Why Do You Need Sleep?* and *Just Listen*

Use a toy clock to help children "count out" the hours from their bedtime until their getting-up time. In this way, they can see how many hours of sleep they are getting.

You might read to children *Sleep Is for Everyone* by Paul Showers (T. Y. Crowell)— a book full of good information. By way of contrast, read the humorous story *Bedtime for Frances* by Russell Hoban (Harper).

90-91 *Why Do You Need Exercise?*

Children will be fascinated by the picture of the skeletal muscles that cover the skeleton—and help us move about. These muscles also hold the bones in place and so hold the body straight.

By feeling the muscles in the upper arm when the elbow is bent, youngsters can get an idea of the shape of these long muscles. They have a thick middle part but become smaller toward each end.

92-95 *Why Can You Move as You Do?*

Muscles help us move about. We can also move as we do because of our joints. Invite boys and girls to demonstrate how they would walk about if they had just bones and no joints—or how they would pick up things if they had no joints in their fingers.

Explain that there are spaces between each of the small bones in the backbone filled with little pads that are something like bone, but are softer. The pads absorb shock when the body moves. They keep the bones from knocking against each other.

96-97 *Just Look*

Boys and girls can be artists too—and can draw or paint pictures of themselves playing favorite games.

98-99 *Why Should You Wash Your Hands?*

In the discussion mention the desirability of using one's own washcloth and towel. Ask, "What is done at school to help you wash your hands well?" (Soap, warm water, and paper towels are made available.)

100-101 *Why Should You Go to the Doctor When You're Not Sick?*

Boys and girls at seven or so should have a checkup, if possible, about once a year— or as often as their doctor suggest. Shots— or preparations given by mouth such as polio vaccine—protect us against such diseases as polio, whooping cough, and measles.

102-103 *How Should You Watch TV?*

Ask for *reasons* for the suggestions given. For instance, when we get a better picture we avoid tiring the eyes. Also our eyes tire more rapidly when the bright light on the TV screen is surrounded by darkness—so we need to have some other light on in the room. The whole body gets tired if we sit hour after hour watching TV; what is more, the exercise we need may be neglected if too much time is spent watching TV.

For more about consumer education, you might refer to the booklet *Early Childhood Consumer Education* by the Project Staff of the Consumers Union of the U.S., Inc.

104-105 *When Do Your New Teeth Come In?*

If possible, make available some small mirrors and toothpicks so children can count in their mouths with a toothpick and note where the six-year molars have grown in. (They are the sixth teeth back from the center of the mouth.)

106-107 *How Should You Take Care of Your Teeth?*

Children might enjoy singing "This is the way we brush our teeth, brush our teeth, brush our teeth; this is the way we brush our teeth so early in the morning" to the tune of "The Mulberry Bush." As they sing, they can also pantomime the back-and-forth brushing motions.

108 *Health Around Us*

See if children can mention the names of other health workers in the community such as doctors, hospital and school nurses, ambulance attendants, dentists, dental hygienists.

A book children can read is *Doctors and Nurses: What Do They Do?* by Carla Greene (Harper).

109 *Do You Remember?*

Some other things you might review with pupils that were stressed in *Book One* pertain to mental health. Thus, you might ask, "How can you show love for others?" and "What things do you like about yourself?"

110 *Things to Do*

Discuss with pupils things about health that they *first* learned about from their families. (How to take a bath, how to shampoo the hair, how to brush the teeth, how to choose clothes to go with the weather, and what foods to eat.)

Ask, "Why is your family important to you?" (Children need a family to care for them, to give them a home and food and clothes.)

111 *Can You Show What You Know?*

Have students react to this situation: "Your little brother or sister wants everything advertised on television. What will you tell him or her?"

112 *Yes or No?*

For an informal test you might say a word and invite pupils to tell all the things the word suggests. Some words you might use are: *exercise, sleep, food, teeth, doctor, wash.*

113 *School and Home*

Be sure to encourage children to report back to the group on how their efforts to pleasantly surprise the family were received.

Enrichment Suggestions for Chapter 4
About the Hospital[1]

Overview

Chapter Four serves the dual purpose of preparing youngsters for basic hospital procedures should they ever have to go to a hospital and of satisfying normal curiosity about hospitals in general. Students have the opportunity to accompany a youngster during a short stay at a hospital. Pupils also learn about the veterinarian and his or her work in an animal hospital.

Important Ideas Developed in the Chapter

A hospital is a place where sick or injured people go to be helped back to good health, and is a place where babies are born.

There are highly trained people at the hospital—doctors, nurses, laboratory workers, X-ray technicians, anesthetists, and so on—to give help to those who need it.

There is special equipment for the care of hospital patients, such as carts, X-ray machines, bedpans and urinals, special beds with tilt-up machinery.

Hospital gowns are easy to put on because they open at the back.

In the operating room, doctors and nurses wear caps and masks to help keep the air clean and free of germs.

It is natural to feel a little scared when going to a strange place like a hospital; it is also natural to feel a little lonesome during a hospital stay.

An animal doctor is called a veterinarian.

Behavioral Objectives

See page 135 in the pupil's book where behavioral objectives in the cognitive area are posed directly to pupils.

[1] See page T45 for Reference Materials related to this chapter.

See also some hoped-for objectives, mainly in the affective area, set forth in the "Teacher's Notes" for page 135.

114–115 *About the Hospital* (Chapter-Opening Pages)

Use the questions on this page to stimulate children to raise the questions they have about hospitals. You might record the children's questions on the chalkboard.

A book children will enjoy hearing you read to them is *Curious George Goes to the Hospital* by Hans A. and Margret Rey.

116–117 *What Happened to Bobby?*

Discuss the fact that Bobby felt a little scared as he was being taken to the hospital. Assure boys and girls that we all feel scared at times when we face new situations and when we are hurt. It helps at these times to have friends or family members, or a doctor or nurse, to reassure us.

118–119 *What Is an X-ray Picture?*

You might write on the chalkboard some of the new words children are learning in this chapter. Some of the words on this page are *intern*, *X ray*, *doctor*. Words from preceding pages are *hospital*, *emergency room*, *cart*.

The hospital worker who takes the X-ray picture of Bobby's leg is an *X-ray technician*. Both men and women may do this work.

120–121 *What Did the Doctor Say?*

To further illustrate the purpose of the cast, show youngsters a broken stick. Ask them to pretend it is a broken bone. Then put the broken ends together and wrap them with some tape. Comment, "The tape does what a cast does. It holds the broken ends in place. The ends of a broken bone gradually mend as they are being held in place.''

122-123 What Is a Hospital Gown?

Youngsters may wonder what will be done with the clothes Bobby wore to the hospital. Explain that his mother or the nurse will take them to the room where Bobby will stay. There the clothes will be put in a closet or in the drawers of a chest. When Bobby is ready to go home, the clothes will be there.

124-125 Who Helps at the Hospital?

Youngsters who have had a drop of their blood taken for tests during a visit to the doctor's office—or during a hospital stay— may want to tell about it.

126-127 What Happened in the Operating Room?

Mention that the anesthetist gives just enough gas to put a person to sleep for the time needed to set a bone or perform an operation. Then the person wakes up just as he or she does from a normal sleep. He or she may feel a little sleepy, though.

128-129 What Happened in Bobby's Room?

Children may be interested in how the button works that Bobby can push to call a nurse. The button will turn on a light over the outside door of Bobby's room and at the nurses' desk. A nurse will see the light and come to Bobby's room.

130-131 What Happened the Next Morning?

Ask, "Why do you think Bobby felt a little lonely when he first woke up?" (He missed his family; he felt a little strange too. It is natural to feel lonely at times when we are away from our families and haven't yet made friends with those around us.)

132-133 Who Visited Bobby?

See if youngsters can infer some other kinds of workers, besides those mentioned in this account, that would be needed in a hospital. (Cooks, clerks, laundry workers, cleaning people, and so on.)

Ask, "What do you think Bobby will tell his friends about the hospital?"

134 Things to Do

Encourage children to make up riddles about workers at a hospital. Or children might pretend they have been in a hospital, like Bobby, and might tell what they liked there, what they didn't like, what they had seen there, and so on.

135 Can You Show What You Know?

A class scrapbook called At the Hospital might include the pictures children draw and any stories they write about workers at the hospital.

136 Yes or No?

For an informal checkup, say a word and invite children to tell all the things the word suggests. Some words you might use are these: intern, X-ray picture, hospital gown, emergency room, recovery room, operating room.

137 School and Home

To further school-home communication, you might use the consumable Activity Booklet designed to accompany this text.

Enrichment Suggestions for Chapter 5
About You and Your World[1]

Overview

Chapter Five focuses on conservation of electricity, water, and paper. Youngsters become aware of the need to avoid litter, to keep picnic places tidy and inviting, to put paper towels in washroom wastebaskets, to make minimal use of pesticides, and to try to reduce noise pollution.

Important Ideas Developed in the Chapter

To save electricity, turn off radios and television sets when they are not in use.

Paper can and should be saved by such means as using both sides of a sheet of paper.

Paper is made from trees; the more paper we use, the more trees must be cut down.

Water is not available in unlimited amounts, so we must learn to use this natural resource wisely.

Bathtubs do not need to be filled too full when one is taking a bath; by using small amounts of water, people can help conserve this natural resource.

We should try to keep picnic places clean and tidy for others to use. After a picnic, we should put our trash in trash cans.

Paper towels should be placed in wastebaskets in school washrooms—not thrown on the floor.

Water spilled on the floor should be wiped up at once so no one will slip and fall.

Bug sprays can be dangerous; they should be used only if necessary, by adults, and in minimal amounts.

Some loud noises can bother people and make them feel tired and cross.

We should try to reduce noise.

[1] See page T46 for Reference Materials related to this chapter.

Behavioral Objectives

See page 159 in the pupil's book where behavioral objectives in the cognitive area are posed directly to pupils.

See also some hoped-for objectives, mainly in the affective area, set forth in the "Teacher's Notes" for page 159.

138–139 *About You and Your World*
            (Chapter-Opening Pages)

Use the questions on these pages to explore youngsters' ideas of what *they* can do to improve life in the world around them.

140–142 *How Can You Help?* and *What Should You Do About the TV?*

Youngsters may be interested in knowing that people have to *pay* for electricity. See if any of the children know that there are meters—in basements or on the outsides of homes—that measure the amount of electricity used. Each family receives a bill monthly or every other month for that amount.

Help students list things in homes that require electricity for their use—TV sets, radios, toasters, air-conditioning units, refrigerators, washing machines, and so on.

142–144 *What Should You Do About a Paper Waster?*

From time to time, pupils can check the wastebasket in the classroom to look for signs that paper is being wasted. Has someone thrown away a piece of paper with writing on just one side?

144–146 *How Much Water Do You Need?*

Invite pupils' cooperation in checking faucets in school washrooms to see that they are turned off completely.

146–148 *What Should You Do with Picnic Trash?*

You and your pupils might check the playground and the school hall for litter. Children can pick up any *paper* litter they find. Items such as broken glass should be picked up by an adult wearing canvas gloves.

148–150 *Where Do You Put the Paper Towel?*

Consider other places at school where liquids might be spilled. What provisions are there for wiping up such spilled liquids?

150–152 *What Should You Do About a Fly?*

Alert pupils to advertisements on television or radio about buying bug sprays. Remind youngsters that the "ad" is planned to make people think they need the bug sprays, and people must learn to decide for themselves about such things.

153–154 *How Should You Play a Radio?*

Ask children to be very quiet and to listen for sounds they hear—perhaps a class singing in a nearby room, horns honking on the street, or shouts from the playground. Invite comments about which sounds are pleasant, which are bothersome, which could be cut down, and so on.

Be sure to discuss the concept that some loud sounds that might be irritating are nevertheless essential. These include fire, police, and ambulance sirens; burglar alarms; warning devices; and so on.

155 *Just Write*

Try to display pupils' writing on bulletin boards or in class scrapbooks. Be sure to display all the pupils' papers. If necessary, have youngsters make second drafts.

156–157 *Health Around Us*

Explore youngsters' ideas about where the water they use comes from. Does it come from a nearby lake? From a river? From deep underground wells? Is it collected in reservoirs far away and sent to the community by huge underground pipes? How could this information be obtained if no one knows? (Parents or neighbors might be consulted. Or the class might write a letter to the local water department.)

158 *Things to Do*

Boys and girls might make simple posters to remind others not to litter. Permission to display posters throughout the school building should be obtained. Also children might make litter bags for the car.

159 *Can You Show What You Know?*

Youngsters might draw pictures of themselves saving water or electricity or paper.

160 *Yes or No?*

For an informal checkup, have students tell all the things these words suggest: *litter, electricity, water, paper, noise.*

161 *School and Home*

Children might also talk over at home ways that are used to cut down on noise. For example, the floors may be carpeted.

162 *Do You Use What You Know?* (End-of-Book Test)

Another review query is: "How do you try to save electricity?"

Chapter One: About You

Books for Children

Anglund, Joan Walsh. *Love Is a Special Way of Feeling.* Harcourt, 1960. A warm little book about various ways of showing love.

Charlip, Remy, and Moore, Lilian. *Hooray for Me!* Parents' Magazine Press, 1975. Well-illustrated book that gives a good feeling about self and others.

Kimmel, Margaret Mary. *Magic in the Mist.* Atheneum, 1975. A fable of kindness to animals.

Raynor, Dorka. *This Is My Father and Me.* A. Whitman, 1973. Lovely black-and-white photographs of fathers and sons in various places throughout the world. Minimum text.

Rinkoff, Barbara. *Red Light Says Stop!* Lothrop, 1974. A fascinating book about "body language" —how we can express ideas without talking. Thus, a shrug, a banged door, a smile all "tell" us something.

Robinson, Tom D. *An Eskimo Birthday.* Dodd, Mead, 1975. An Eskimo girl feels the love of her family on her birthday. A read-aloud book.

Rudolph, Marguerita. *The Sneaky Machine.* McGraw-Hill, 1974. Henry loves his grandmother and likes to help her vacuum, but becomes unhappy when his friends call vacuuming "mommy's work."

Tompert, Ann. *Little Otter Remembers and Other Stories.* Crown, 1977. Little Otter experiences joy, sorrow, and disappointment.

Wells, Rosemary. *Abdul.* Dial, 1975. A camel gives birth to a colt, but will not abandon him even if he is different.

Materials for Teachers and Parents[1]

Bower, Eli. *Teachers Talk About Their Feelings.* National Institute of Health, Center for Studies of Child and Family Health, 1973. Unusual account of the feelings of some young teachers during their first days in the classroom.

Jenkins, Gladys Gardner, and Schacter, Helen S. *These Are Your Children.* 4th ed. Scott, Foresman, 1975. A highly readable book on child growth and development.

National Association for Mental Health, Inc. *What Every Child Needs.* NAMH. Effective leaflet on the emotional needs of children.

Films and Filmstrips[2] for Classroom Use

Be Healthy! Be Happy! (Perennial, produced by Portafilms).

Getting Angry (BFA Educational Media)

How Do You Know You're Growing Up? (ABC Media Concepts).

Making Mistakes (Scholastic).

Nothing Ever Seems to Work Out for Me (Britannica Films).

Oops, I Made a Mistake! (Britannica Films).

Chapter Two: About Your Senses and Your Safety

Books for Children

Aliki. *My Five Senses.* T. Y. Crowell, 1962. A very simple first book on the senses.

Kessler, Leonard. *A Tale of Two Bicycles: Safety on Your Bike.* Lothrop, 1971. Bicycle riders see what can happen in a short time to two new bicycles and their riders.

Rey, Hans A. *Curious George Rides a Bike.* Houghton, 1952. The adventures of this lively monkey clarify the need for bicycle safety.

Showers, Paul. *Find Out by Touching.* T. Y. Crowell, 1961.
_____. *The Listening Walk.* T. Y. Crowell, 1961.
_____. *Follow Your Nose.* T. Y. Crowell, 1963.
_____. *Look at Your Eyes.* T. Y. Crowell, 1962.
_____. *Your Skin and Mine.* T. Y. Crowell, 1965.
Five easy-to-read but very informative books.

---

[1] See also specialized reading lists on pages T24, T27, and T29.
[2] Filmstrips are marked with an asterisk.

Materials for Teachers and Parents[1]
National Safety Council. *All About Fire Safety, Vol. 1.* NSC, 1977. Contains teacher's notes and spirit master activity sheets.

National Safety Council. Safety Education Data Sheets: *Matches, Falls, Pedestrian Safety, Play Areas, Playground Apparatus, School Bus Safety, School Fire Safety.* NSC. Excellent enrichment material on the various topics listed.

Thygerson, Alton L. *Safety: Principles, Instruction, and Readings.* Prentice-Hall, 1972. Useful sourcebook on all aspects of safety education.

Films and Filmstrips[2] for Classroom Use
Bicycle Riding Reminders (Aims).

Drugs: A Primary Film (Arthur Barr Productions, Inc.).

The Five Senses (Britannica Films).

*The Five Senses (Scott Education Division). A series of five filmstrips: *Look How You See; Here's Your Ear; How Your Nose Knows; Your Tasting Tongue;* and *The Feel of Your Skin.*

Learning with Your Senses (Coronet).

Look, Listen, and Learn (ABC Media Concepts).

Pedestrian Signs and Signals (Aims).

Pigs! (Dimension Films for Churchill). Motivates children to use their eyes and ears.

Safety: Home Safe Home (Aims).

Safety Rules for School (Aims).

The Simple Accident (Sid Davis).

Chapter Three: About Your Health Questions

Books for Children
Cobb, Vicki. *How the Doctor Knows You're Fine.* Lippincott, 1973. A reassuring account of what happens in a health checkup.

Cultice, Virginia C. *Kivi Speaks.* Lothrop, 1975. An Eskimo boy tells, in poetry, of a time of hunger and of his people's joy when the hunters finally catch a walrus.

Frahm, Anne. *The True Book of Bacteria.* Childrens Press, 1963. A simple introduction to bacteria.

Hoban, Russell. *Bread and Jam for Frances.* Harper, 1964. Children enjoy reading about Frances who, for a time, wanted to eat only bread and jam.

Kessler, Leonard. *On Your Mark, Get Set, Go!* Harper, 1972. A Sports I CAN READ Book.

Lionni, Leo. *In the Rabbitgarden.* Pantheon, 1975. Delightfully illustrated book about some rabbits that try a new food.

Rockwell, Harlow. *My Doctor.* Macmillan, 1973. Easy-to-read, well-illustrated book on a visit to a doctor. The doctor is a woman.

Showers, Paul. *Sleep Is for Everyone.* T. Y. Crowell, 1974. An excellent book, full of information and a discussion of what would happen if you *never* went to bed.

Wahl, Jan. *The Clumpets Go Sailing.* Parents' Magazine Press, 1975. The Clumpets go out of their way to bring food to an ailing relative.

Young, Helen. *Wide-Awake Jake.* Morrow, 1975. When Jake can't sleep, his mother poses an interesting solution.

Materials for Teachers and Parents[1]
American Dental Association. *Cleaning Your Teeth and Gums* and *Happiness Is a Healthy Mouth.* ADA. Basic, up-to-date information on toothbrushing and flossing is provided in these booklets.

Boston Children's Medical Center. *Child Health Encyclopedia.* Delacorte, 1975. Written and indexed for use by parents.

---

[1] See also specialized reading lists on pages T24, T27, and T29.
[2] Filmstrips are marked with an asterisk.

Levine, Milton I., and Seligmann, Jean H. *The Parents' Encyclopedia of Infancy, Childhood, and Adolescence.* T. Y. Crowell, 1973. A storehouse of sound, useful information on all aspects of child growth and development.

National Dairy Council. *Animals That Give People Milk* and *The Four Food Groups.* NDC. A booklet and a poster with accompanying activity piece.

Films for Classroom Use
Foods Around Us (Britannica Films)

Foods from Grains (Coronet).

Germs and What They Do (Coronet).

Health—Exercise, Rest, and Sleep (Aims).

How Do You Know You're Growing Up? (ABC Media Concepts).

Stanley Takes a Trip (National Film Board of Canada).

Chapter Four: About the Hospital

Books for Children
Greene, Carla. *Animal Doctors: What Do They Do?* Harper, 1967. An appealing account of the veterinarian's work.

Hefflefinger, Jane, and Hoffman, Elaine. *At the Pet Hospital.* Childrens Press, 1964. Children can easily read this book.

Iritani, Chika. *I Know an Animal Doctor.* Putnam, 1971. One of a series of Community Helper Books.

Kay, Eleanor, R.N. *Let's Find Out About Hospitals.* Watts, 1971. Excellent descriptions of what goes on at a hospital.

Meeker, Alice M. *How Hospitals Help Us.* Benefic, 1962. Information for primary-age youngsters.

Rey, Hans A., and Rey, Margret. *Curious George Goes to the Hospital.* Houghton, 1966. Children love this exciting tale of Curious George, the monkey, and his misadventures at the hospital.

Sharmat, Marjorie W. *I Want Mama.* Harper, 1974. Easy-to-read, charming story of how a little girl feels when her mother goes to the hospital to have an operation.

Shay, Arthur. *What Happens When You Go to the Hospital.* Reilly & Lee, 1969. A black girl goes to the hospital to have her tonsils out.

Sobol, Harriet Langsam. *Jeff's Hospital Book.* Walck, 1975. Describes a young boy's experience in the hospital as he undergoes surgery to correct crossed eyes.

Materials for Teachers and Parents[1]
Haller, J. Alex, Jr., M.D.; Talbert, James L., M.D.; and Dombro, Robert H. *The Hospitalized Child and His Family.* Johns Hopkins Press, 1967. Series of essays on ways to lessen the traumatic effects of a stay in the hospital.

X-ray pictures of various bones and body organs can often be obtained free for educational purposes from a community hospital. These X-ray pictures can be taped to the classroom window for observation.

Films for Classroom Use
Drugs: A Primary Film (Arthur Barr Productions, Inc.)

The Veterinarian Serves the Community (Aims, produced by Films/West).

Chapter Five: About You and Your World

Books for Children
Chapin, Cynthia. *Clean Streets, Clean Water, Clean Air.* A. Whitman, 1970. Easy-to-read book with focus on what people can do to improve their environment.

Gans, Roma. *Water for Dinosaurs and You.* T. Y. Crowell, 1972. Easy-to-read book explains the water cycle and shows what happens when pollutants enter the water.

---

[1] See also specialized reading lists on pages T24, T27, and T29.

Hallinan, P. K. *The Looking Book*. Childrens Press, 1973. A charming story about two children who turned off the TV and went out to explore the wonders of the world around them.

Hazen, Barbara S. *World, World, What Can I Do?* Abingdon, 1976. A child reflects on what can be done to improve the environment.

Leaf, Munro. *Who Cares? I Do*. Lippincott, 1971. Shows what spoilers, droppers, and wreckers can do to our environment.

Paola, Tomie de. *Michael Bird-Boy*. Prentice-Hall, 1975. Michael encourages respect for the environment as he follows a dark cloud to its source.

Pounds, Elenore T., and others. Health and Growth Enrichment Booklets: *Noise, Noise, Noise; Once There Was a River: A Story of Water Polution; Wastebasket Full, Wastebasket Empty;* and *Who Cares About Air Pollution?* Scott, Foresman, 1974. Photographs in color add to the simply written materials on environmental health.

Radlauer, Edward, and Radlauer, Ruth. *Water for Your Community*. Childrens Press, 1968. Advanced readers will find good materials on why we need water, where we get it, and how we can save it.

Rockwell, Harlow. *The Compost Heap*. Doubleday, 1972. A simply written picture book to show children one way to save things and use them again in another form.

Simon, Seymour. *Water on Your Street*. Holiday House, 1974. Simple story about where water comes from and where it goes.

Materials for Teachers and Parents
Johnny Horizon News Bureau. *Small Steps in the Right Direction. Information Sheets 1 and 2.* Order from the Nationwide Environmental Action and Awareness Campaign, The President's Council on Environmental Quality, Department of the Interior, Washington, D.C. 20240.

Sale, Larry L., and Lee, Ernest W. *Environmental Education in the Elementary School*. Holt, 1972. A helpful textbook to help teachers plan environmental-education experiences for children.

U.S. Environmental Protection Agency. *Fun with the Environment*. U.S. Government Printing Office, 1973 (75 cents). A booklet for children that teachers and parents will find useful too.

Films for Classroom Use
Community Helpers: The Sanitation Department (Aims).

Health: You and Your Helpers (Aims).

Water for the City (BFA Educational Media).

Teacher's Questionnaire *You and Your Health*

Please complete this questionnaire after you have finished teaching the **new** Scott, Foresman HEALTH Program for the school year. Remove the questionnaire from the book, fold it as shown, staple it, and place it in the nearest mailbox. No postage is required.

1. How would you identify the overall ability of the children in your class?

    EMH or TMH ☐ Below average ☐ Average ☐ Above average ☐ Gifted ☐

2. Was the text an effective teaching tool? Why or why not? _____
   _____
   _____

3. What is your opinion of the readability? _____
   _____

4. How useful are the illustrations in helping students learn? _____
   _____

5. Did any parts of the text cause learner difficulty? _____
   _____
   _____

6. What improvements would you suggest? _____
   _____
   _____

7. What health questions do your pupils ask most often? _____
   _____
   _____

8. Indicate which features of the text you like and which features you do not like.

Like	Don't Like		Like	Don't Like	
☐	☐	Chapter Opening Pages	☐	☐	Health Around Us
☐	☐	Just Listen	☐	☐	Things to Do
☐	☐	Just Look	☐	☐	Can You Show What You Know?
☐	☐	Just Sing	☐	☐	Chapter Test
☐	☐	Just Write	☐	☐	School and Home

9. Indicate which features of the *Teacher's Edition* you like and which features you do not like.

Like	Don't Like		Like	Don't Like	
☐	☐	Teacher's Notes	☐	☐	A Healthful Classroom Environment
☐	☐	Family-Life Education	☐	☐	Signs & Symptoms of Illness
☐	☐	Enrichment Suggestions	☐	☐	The Parent-Teacher Conference
☐	☐	Reference Materials	☐	☐	If Children Ask About Death
☐	☐	A Developmental Profile of Seven- to Eight-Year-Olds	☐	☐	Movement Exploration and Games
			☐	☐	The "How" of Health Teaching

If you would be willing to complete a questionnaire after teaching the program for another year, please fill in your return address.

Name_____

School_____

Address_____

City_____ State_____ Zip Code_____

Fold on dotted line so return address and mailing address are on outside of questionnaire.

School, Home, Community

You and Your Health

Teacher's Notes

In this *Teacher's Edition* "Teacher's Notes" are overprinted on the pupil's pages.

Words to Know listed after *Vocabulary Development* at the beginning of each chapter are in the order that they appear in the text.

With the exception of specialized health and safety words, this book is written chiefly in the vocabulary of well-known vocabulary lists for first-grade and early second-grade levels. The pupil's text has been kept easy so that all seven- to eight-year-olds can enjoy health and safety material "custom built" for their special health needs and interests.

Julius B. Richmond, M.D.
Elenore T. Pounds, M.A.

In consultation with
Orvis A. Harrelson, M.D., M.P.H.
Gladys Gardner Jenkins, M.A.
Wallace Ann Wesley, Hs.D.

Scott, Foresman and Company
Editorial Offices: Glenview, Illinois
Regional Sales Offices: Palo Alto, California •
Tucker, Georgia • Glenview, Illinois •
Oakland, New Jersey • Dallas, Texas

Authors

Julius B. Richmond, M.D. Professor of Child Psychiatry and Human Development and Professor and Chairman, Department of Social and Preventive Medicine, Harvard Medical School; Director, Judge Baker Guidance Center; Chief of Psychiatric Service, Children's Hospital Medical Center, Boston, Massachusetts.

Elenore T. Pounds, M.A. Writer; lecturer; former Directing Editor of the Health and Personal Development Program; classroom teacher; coauthor of the *Health and Growth* Program; author of *Drugs and Your Safety* and other *Health Enrichment Booklets.*

Consultants

Orvis A. Harrelson, M.D., M.P.H. Corporate Medical Director, Weyerhauser Company, Tacoma, Washington; former Administrative Director of Health, Tacoma Public Schools, Tacoma, Washington.

Gladys Gardner Jenkins, M.A. Lecturer in Parent-Child-Teacher Relationships, University of Iowa, Iowa City, Iowa; former member, National Advisory Council on Child Growth and Human Development; author of *Helping Children Reach Their Potential;* coauthor of *These Are Your Children.*

Wallace Ann Wesley, Hs.D. Director, Department of Health Education, American Medical Association, Chicago, Illinois; former teacher at primary through college levels.

ISBN: 0-673-11038-9

345678910 WAK 898887868584838281

Content Specialists

Richard H. Blum, Ph.D. Consulting Professor, Department of Psychology and Director, Joint Program in Drugs, Crime, and Community Studies, Center for Interdisciplinary Research, Stanford University, Stanford, California.

Willie D. Ford, Ph.D. Professor, Nutrition and Home Economics, Grambling State University, Grambling, Louisiana; former Nutrition Specialist, U.S. Department of Agriculture, University of Nebraska, Lincoln, Nebraska.

Lucia Guzman, B.S. Assistant to the Dean for Student Affairs, University of Texas School of Allied Health Sciences, University of Texas Medical Branch, Galveston, Texas.

Barbara J. Kohuth, B.S. Environmental Health Educator; Head, Office of Environmental Education and Public Information, Cleveland Department of Public Health and Welfare, Cleveland, Ohio.

Boyd T. Marsh, M.A., B.S. Deputy Health Commissioner for Environmental Health, Cleveland Department of Public Health and Welfare, Cleveland, Ohio.

Norman H. Olsen, D.D.S. Chairman of the Department of Pedodontics and Dean of The Dental School, Northwestern University, Chicago, Illinois.

Marguerite Robinson, M.S. Consumer Specialist, Department of Health, Education, Welfare, Food and Drug Administration, Chicago, Illinois; Past President, Chicago Nutrition Association, Chicago, Illinois.

Joan Tillotson, Ph.D. Consultant in Movement Education, The University of North Carolina at Charlotte, Charlotte, North Carolina.

Wilma Yee, B.S., R.N. Public Health Nurse and School Nurse, Oakland Public Schools, Oakland, California.

The assistance of the National Safety Council, Chicago, Illinois, in reviewing the safety advice in this material is gratefully acknowledged.

Learner Feedback

Experimental versions of many of the lessons in the YOU AND YOUR HEALTH Program for the primary grades were used during the 1975-1976 school year with students at Levy Elementary School, Torrance, California; Mayport Elementary School, Atlantic Beach, Florida; St. Mary's School, Darien, Illinois; and Public School 276, Brooklyn, New York. The authors and editors of the program are grateful to the students and to the teachers in these schools for their comments and their suggestions.

Contents

I About You

What is special about you?
What are some feelings you have?

Teacher's Notes
See the Enrichment Suggestions for
Chapter One on pages T30–T32. See
also suggested Reference Materials on
page T43.

Vocabulary Development The
following words are included in the
vocabulary for Chapter 1: *special,
feelings, happy, unhappy, proud,
kindness, kind, mistakes.* You may
want to introduce these words. Write
them on the board and use each one
in a sentence. Encourage students
to use the words in sentences of
their own. Each chapter will introduce vocabulary words.

Words to Know
feelings
happy
kind
kindness
mistakes
proud
special
unhappy

Are You Just Like Anyone Else?

Suppose you were in this picture. Would you look just like anyone here?

Would you be just like anyone here?
How would you be different?

Teacher's Notes

Invite spontaneous comments on the pictures here. Where did they come from? (Probably class pictures.) Pupils will think of innumerable ways in which each one of them would differ in looks from the pictured children—in height, weight, facial features, eye color or shape, skin color, and so on.

11

Teacher's Notes
Children will enjoy the "Art Gallery"
shown on pages 12 and 13 of some
children's own self-portraits and things
children do well. Once again it is clear
that individuals differ—in the pictures
they draw of themselves as well as in
so many other ways.

Teacher's Notes
Children "just listen" as you read this poem. Later they can read it along with you.
See also page T30 for additional teaching suggestions.

JUST LISTEN

I'm Glad I'm Me

No one looks
The way I do.
I have noticed
That it's true;
   No one walks
   The way I walk.
   No one talks
   The way I talk.
   No one plays
   The way I play.
   No one says
   The things I say.
I am special.
I am me.
There's no one
I'd rather be
   than
      me!

How are you special?

"I'm Glad I'm Me" is to read to the children as they just listen.

"I'm Glad I'm Me" by Ruth Dana Pedersen. Reprinted from *One/Two*, September 3, 1972. Copyright © 1972 by Graded Press.

13

How Are You Like Others?

You are different from others
in many ways.
But you are like others too.

Teacher's Notes
Youngsters have been talking about
how each of them is different from
others. Now they begin to consider
some basic human likenesses. An
important one is the universality of
human emotions and needs.
Have pupils identify what emotions
are being expressed by the children
shown on this page and page 15.

14

You have feelings.
Others have feelings.
What feelings do we all have?

Teacher's Notes
Stress again the idea that it isn't only children who experience emotions such as anger, fear, joy, and so on. *Everyone*—fathers, mothers, teachers, grandparents—has these emotions from time to time.
See also page T31 for additional teaching suggestions.

How Do You Feel at School?

Sometimes you feel one way.
Sometimes you feel another way.
Everyone is like that.

What can make you feel happy at school?
What makes you feel unhappy?
What makes you feel proud?

How Do You Show Kindness?

Do you show kindness to others?
Do you like others to be kind
to you?

Teacher's Notes
Pages 18 and 19 can start off rich
discussion and dramatic portrayal of
ways in which we can express kindly
feelings toward others.

18

Just what is kindness?
Act out a way to show kindness.
How does kindness make you feel?

Teacher's Notes
Supplement the discussion of the questions and the dramatic skits with consideration of:
"How would *you* tell someone what kindness is?"
Write youngsters' responses on the chalkboard or on a group chart.

19

How Does It Feel to Make Mistakes?

Linda made some mistakes one day.
She made some mistakes
in spelling.

How do you think she felt?

How do you feel when you make
mistakes?

Teacher's Notes

Children of seven or so are apt to take mistakes very seriously. They may feel ashamed or worried; they may think that people shouldn't make mistakes, that there is something wrong with people who do make them. Pages 20 and 21 are designed to stress the fact that we all make mistakes at times; we may not like to, but we do. It is no disgrace to make mistakes when you have tried as best you can; we can learn from our mistakes.

Discuss all the questions asked in the pupil's text on pages 20 and 21.

See page T31 for additional teaching suggestions.

We all make mistakes.
But we can learn from mistakes.
Then we may not make them again.
What can Linda learn from her mistakes?
Think of a mistake you made.
What did you learn from it?

JUST SING

Teacher's Notes
Teach this song as you would any other new one. From time to time during the year, come back and review the song. It has a valuable mental-health message.

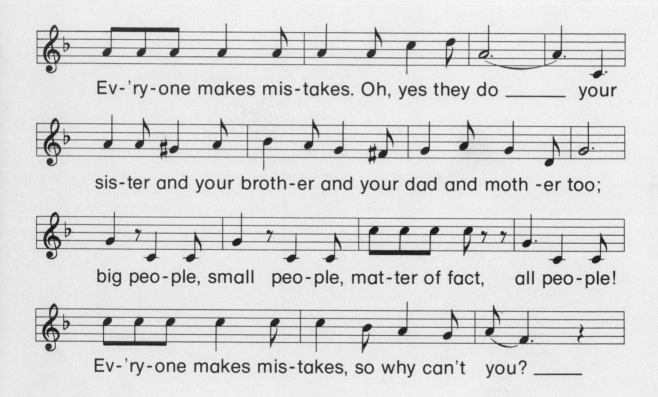

Ev-'ry-one makes mis-takes. Oh, yes they do _____ your

sis-ter and your broth-er and your dad and moth -er too;

big peo-ple, small   peo-ple, mat-ter of fact,   all peo-ple!

Ev-'ry-one makes mis-takes, so why can't   you? _____

JUST LOOK

An artist painted this picture long ago.
How do you think the girl feels?
What might make her feel this way?

Auguste Renoir: *A Girl with a Watering Can*.
National Gallery of Art, Washington, D.C.
Chester Dale Collection.

HEALTH AROUND US

We often see cards and notes.
How do they make people feel?

Teacher's Notes

"Health Around Us" is a recurring feature in this book and in this health series. It focuses on interesting and intriguing aspects of health in the world around us. At times new developments in the field of health will be highlighted.

Here children's attention is focused on a commonplace sight—cards or notes that express feelings of love or thoughtfulness or kindness.

Ask:

"What have *you* written lately that might make someone feel happy?" (A letter to a grandparent, a story just for fun to be read to the group, a get-well message, and so on.)

See page T32 for additional teaching suggestions.

24

Activities

Teacher's Notes
Six special health words used in the chapter are reviewed. An appealing, active way to help children learn to spell the words is also suggested. Using real or "pretend" balls, children "bounce out" a spelling—one bounce for each letter and one bounce for each word chanted. Such rhythmic chants delight young children and help them remember in correct order the letters in a given word.
See also page T32 for additional teaching suggestions.

Things to Do

1. See if you know these health words.

happy   proud

unhappy   kind

feelings   mistakes

2. Try to spell the words you see above.
   Here is a way to help you.

h   a   p   p   y   spells   happy

More Things to Do

Teacher's Notes

Boys and girls will enjoy exploring ways in which they can express the feelings of happiness, anger, and pride through body movements.

In initiating these movement activities, start with volunteers. You might also use a "Follow the Leader" approach. If possible, children might also move to music that suggests such feelings as happiness, excitement, fear.

See page T32 for additional teaching ideas.

Joe

Pete

Ann

1. Look at the pictures.
   Find someone who looks happy.
   Find someone who looks proud.
   Find someone who looks angry.

2. Pretend you feel very happy.
   Show how you would look.
   Show how you would move about.

26

Can You Show What You Know?

1. Tell one way all people are alike.

2. Name some feelings we all have at times.

3. Tell what kindness means to you.

4. Draw a picture of you doing something kind.

5. Act out a way to show kindness.

6. Tell what makes you feel happy.

7. Tell what you should know about mistakes.

8. Tell what you have learned from a mistake.

9. Tell something that is special about you.

Teacher's Notes

Here behavioral objectives in the cognitive area are posed in childlike language directly to the children themselves. In turn, boys and girls give evidence by *observable behavior* of what they have learned.

Other hoped-for behavioral objectives lie chiefly in the less easily observed affective area—objectives that pertain to feelings, attitudes, and values. Some of them are:

Feels comfortable about one's own feelings.

Is aware that each person is unique.

Discovers ways in which all human beings are alike.

Realizes that all people have feelings.

Becomes sensitive to ways in which we can express kindly feelings toward others.

Realizes that everyone makes mistakes and that we can profit from our mistakes if we will.

Discovers ways in which actions or written words can make others feel happy or wanted or missed.

Behavioral objectives in the cognitive area are stated here directly to children themselves.

Yes or No?

Teacher's Notes
This "Yes or No?" exercise is a simple test, presented in a form youngsters enjoy. They look upon it as a sort of puzzle.
Have pupils read each question silently and be ready to tell the answer. Or, if children are able, they might write on their papers each number and after it the correct answer, *yes* or *no*.
Answers to the questions are:
1. no; 2. yes; 3. yes; 4. yes; 5. no; 6. yes; 7. yes; 8. no; 9. yes.

1. Is anyone just like you?

2. Do you sometimes feel happy?

3. Do you sometimes feel unhappy?

4. Do you sometimes feel angry?

5. Do you feel the same way all the time?

6. Can you learn from your mistakes?

7. Can these words make someone feel happy?

   (I love you.)

8. Can these words make someone feel happy?

   (Go away. You can't play.)

9. Can these words make someone feel happy?

   (We miss you.)

SCHOOL & HOME

Teacher's Notes
Special efforts are made in this book
and in this health series to foster
school-home communication. This
page is an example of how youngsters
are encouraged to share with the family
the health ideas they are acquiring at
school. An important mental-health
concept is also presented. When you
are troubled or upset about something,
try talking it over with a parent or
some other grown-up.

(*Note:* Also available from Scott,
Foresman to help further school-home
communication is the consumable
Activity Booklet for your class. See
page T7 for a description of this
booklet.)
See also page T32 for additional
teaching suggestions.

Talk about your feelings with
a grown-up at home.

Talking things over helps you
feel better.

Tell your family about things you
learn at school.

What can you tell about mistakes?

What can you do at home
to show kindness?

2 About Your Senses and Your Safety

What are your five main senses?
How can your senses keep you safe?
What should you know about safety?

Teacher's Notes
See the Enrichment Suggestions for
Chapter Two on pages T33–T35. See
also the suggested Reference Materials
on pages T43–T44.

Vocabulary Development Introduce
the Words to Know: *senses, eyes,
nerves, ears, nose, tongue, skin,
brain.* Other words used in Chapter
2 are *bicycle, fire, hear, medicine,
messages, safety, see, sign, smell,
taste, touch.*

Words to Know
brain
ears
eyes
nerves
nose
senses
skin
tongue

How Do You Know What Goes On Around You?

You have five main senses.
Do you know what they are?
How can these senses help keep you safe?

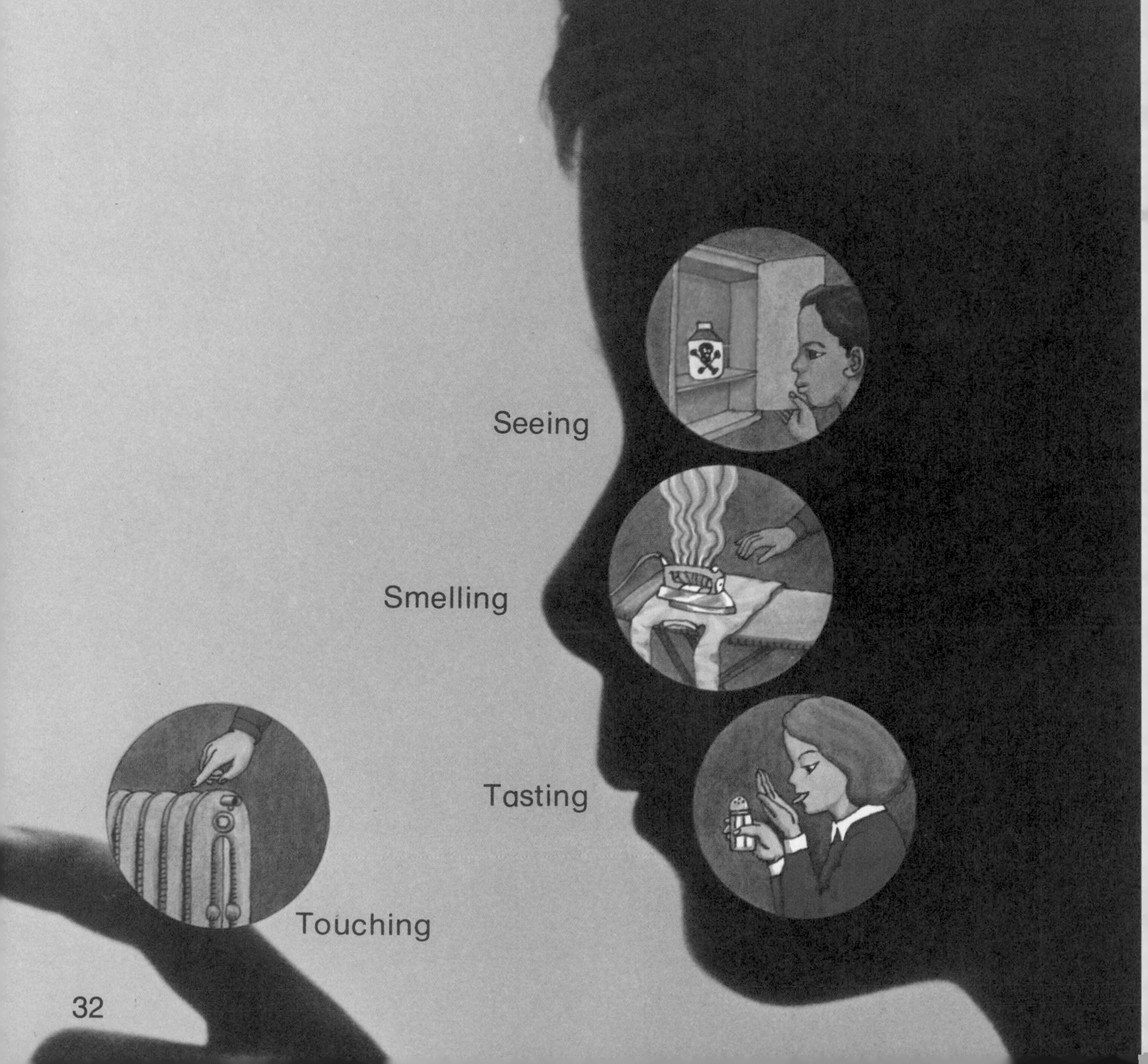

Seeing

Smelling

Tasting

Touching

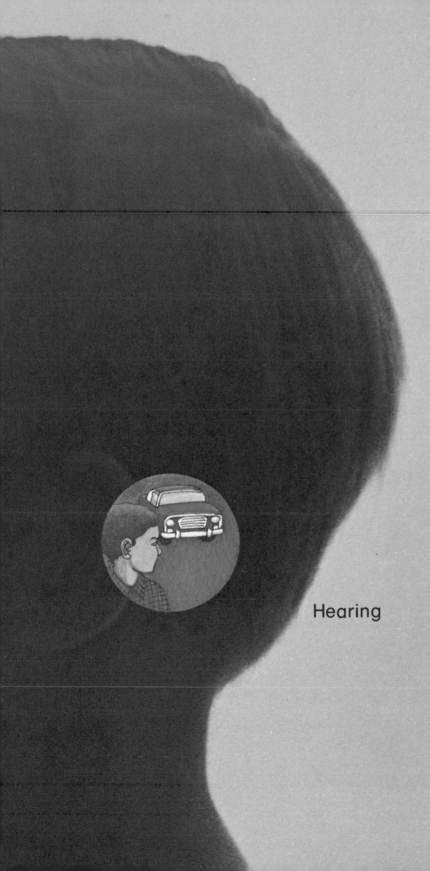

Hearing

33

How Do Your Eyes Help?

You have two eyes for seeing.

You see traffic lights.

You see safety signs.

You see cars coming.

Your eyes send messages about what you see.

The messages go to your brain.

Then you know what you see.

How can this help keep you safe?

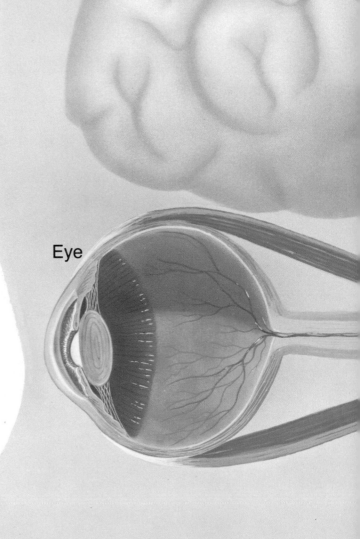

Eye

Brain

Nerve

Teacher's Notes

Invite comments on what the picture on these two pages shows. (It shows some things you would see if you could look inside the head, such as the *eye* at each side of the *brain*.)

Explain that when we look at our eyes, we just see the front of them. But if we could see every part of them, we would see that they are round like a ball. That is why they are called *eyeballs*. There are many different parts of the eye. Each part helps us see. One interesting part is the one that looks like a little black spot in each eye. But it isn't really a spot. It is a round hole that lets light into the eye. The little hole is called a *pupil*. Ask:

"What happens to make you able to see something?" (The eyes carry the message over nerves to your brain; your brain tells you what it is you are seeing. More will be learned about nerves on pages 46 and 47.)

See also the additional helps on page T34.

How Do Your Ears Help?

You have ears for hearing.
You can hear cars honk.
You can hear a train coming.
You can hear a dog bark.
You can hear the fire bell
at school.

Your ears send messages about
what you hear.

The messages go to your brain.
Then you know what you hear.
How can this help keep you safe?

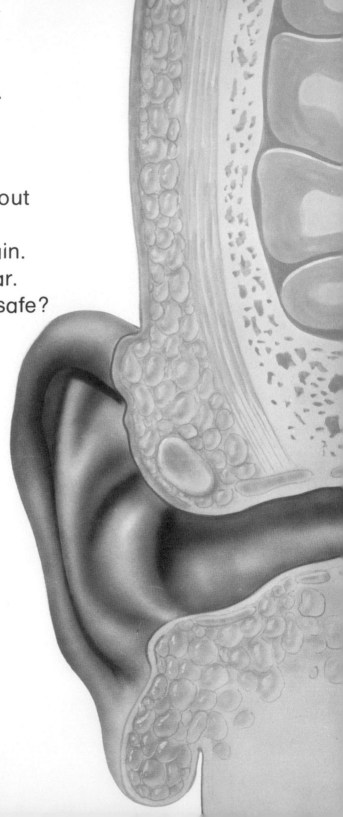

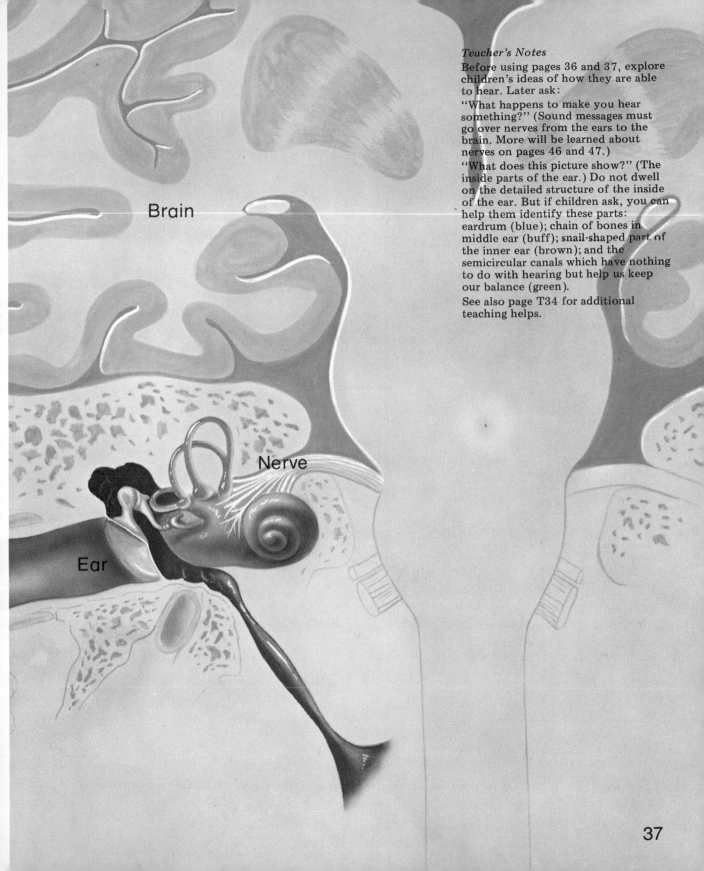

Brain

Nerve

Ear

Teacher's Notes

Before using pages 36 and 37, explore children's ideas of how they are able to hear. Later ask:

"What happens to make you hear something?" (Sound messages must go over nerves from the ears to the brain. More will be learned about nerves on pages 46 and 47.)

"What does this picture show?" (The inside parts of the ear.) Do not dwell on the detailed structure of the inside of the ear. But if children ask, you can help them identify these parts: eardrum (blue); chain of bones in middle ear (buff); snail-shaped part of the inner ear (brown); and the semicircular canals which have nothing to do with hearing but help us keep our balance (green).

See also page T34 for additional teaching helps.

How Does Your Nose Help?

You have a nose for smelling.

You can smell smoke from a fire.

You can smell something burning on the stove.

You can smell some gases that could hurt you.

Your nose sends messages about what you smell.

The messages go to your brain.

Then you know what you smell.

How can this help keep you safe?

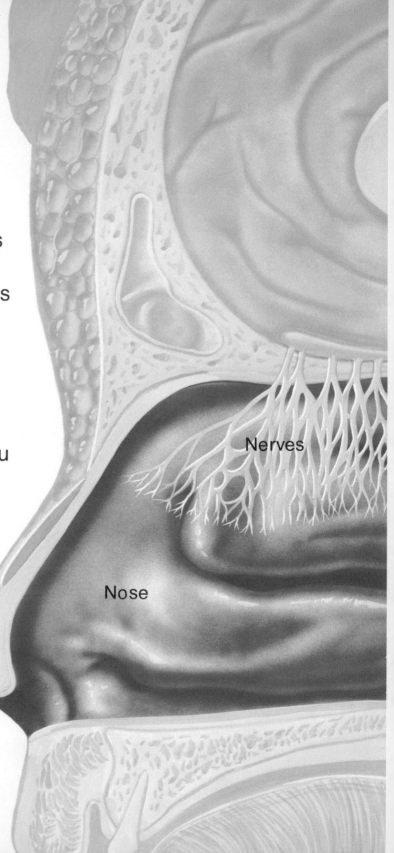

Nerves

Nose

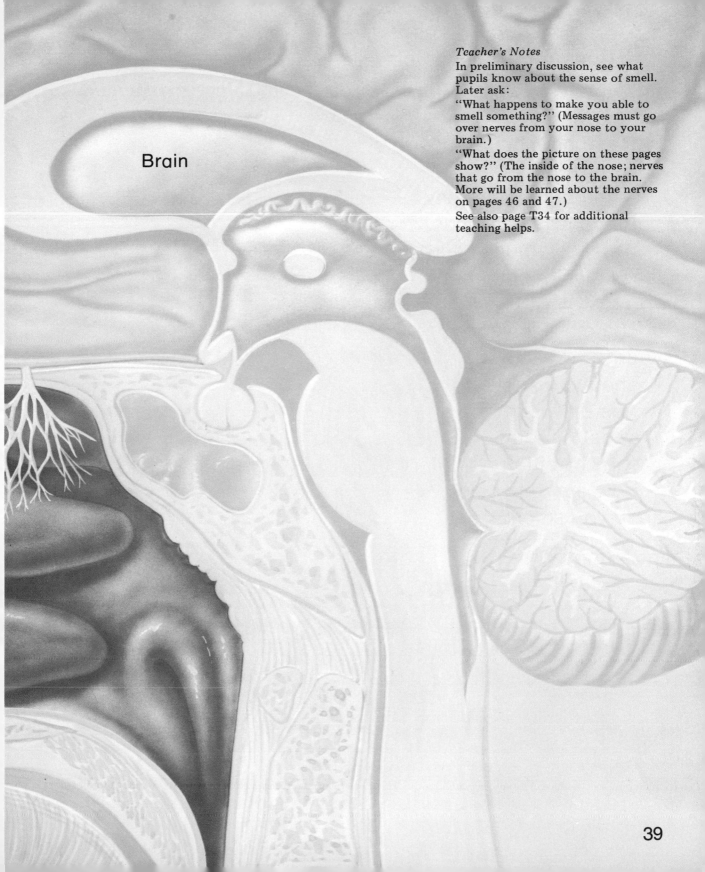

Brain

Teacher's Notes

In preliminary discussion, see what pupils know about the sense of smell. Later ask:

"What happens to make you able to smell something?" (Messages must go over nerves from your nose to your brain.)

"What does the picture on these pages show?" (The inside of the nose; nerves that go from the nose to the brain. More will be learned about the nerves on pages 46 and 47.)

See also page T34 for additional teaching helps.

How Does Your Tongue Help?

You have a tongue for tasting.

There are little bumps on your tongue.

In the bumps are tiny parts called taste buds.

Your taste buds send messages about what you taste.

The messages go to your brain.

Then you know if things are
sweet or sour,
salty or bitter.

How can this help keep you safe?

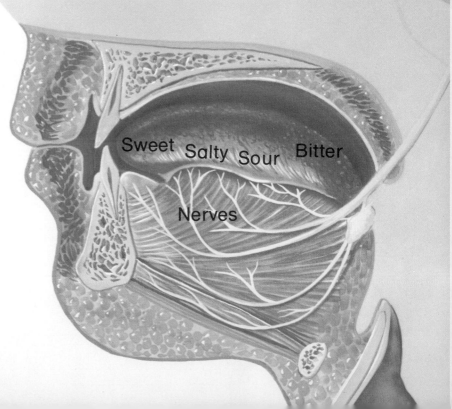

Sweet Salty Sour Bitter

Nerves

Brain

Teacher's Notes
Before using these pages see what ideas
pupils have about how they are able to
taste things. Later ask:

"What happens to make you able to
taste something?" (Messages go from
taste buds over nerves to the brain.)

"What do you see in the picture?" (A
"map" of one side of the tongue—
which, divided into parts, shows what
areas of the tongue have the taste buds
for sweet things, salty things, sour
things, and bitter things; and the
nerves from those areas that lead up
to the brain.)

Children may also want to find the
bony tissues of the jawbone and the
two teeth (shown in cross section).
See also page T34 for additional
teaching helps.

How Do Your Fingers Help?

Your sense of touch is
in your skin.

You have fingers for
touching.

Skin covers the fingers.

In the skin are many tiny
nerves.

They send messages about
what you touch.

The messages go to your
brain.

Then you know if
things are
   hot or cold,
   rough or smooth,
   soft or hard,
   sharp or dull.

How can this help
keep you safe?

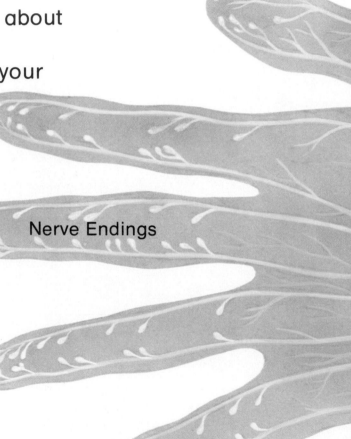

Nerve Endings

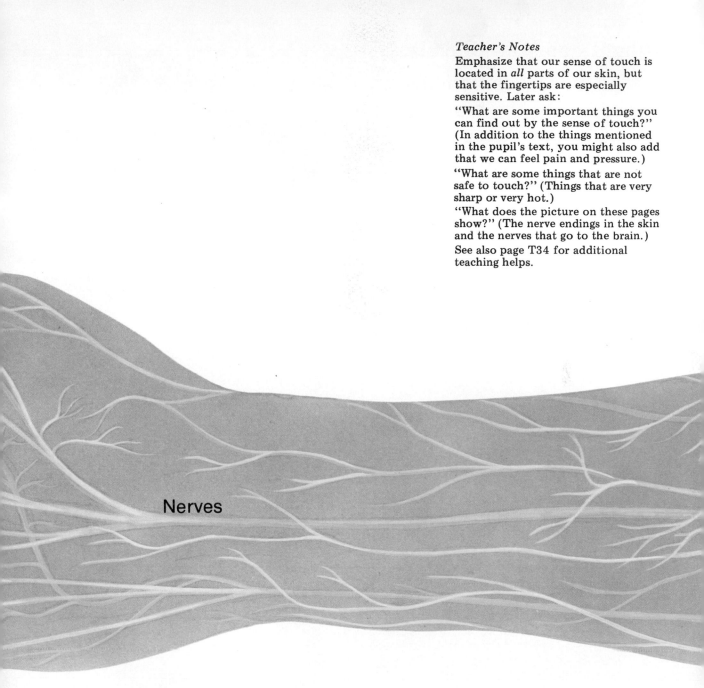

Nerves

What Does Your Brain Do?

The messages from the senses go to the brain.

The brain tells you what they mean.

You think with your brain.

You think about messages from the senses.

You decide what to do.

What happens in your brain when you see a stoplight?

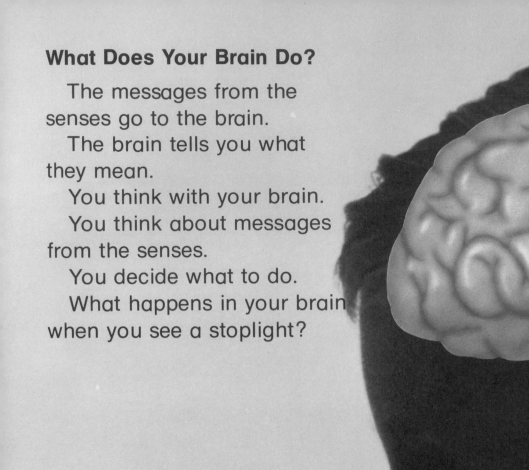

Brain

44

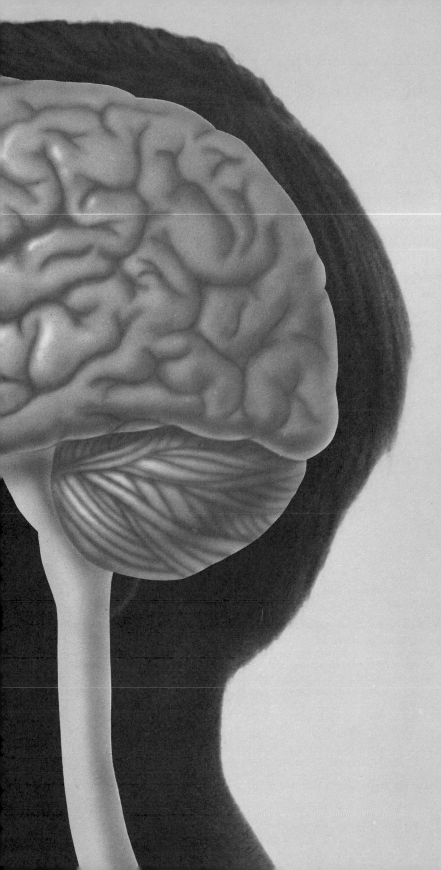

Teacher's Notes
After study of these pages, ask:
"Could you see, hear, touch, taste, or smell without your brain? Why or why not?"
Explain that the brain is surrounded by the bones of the head. These bones are called the *skull*. The picture here does not show the skull. If it did, the brain could not be seen. Children may be encouraged to *feel* their skulls. See also page T34 for additional teaching suggestions.

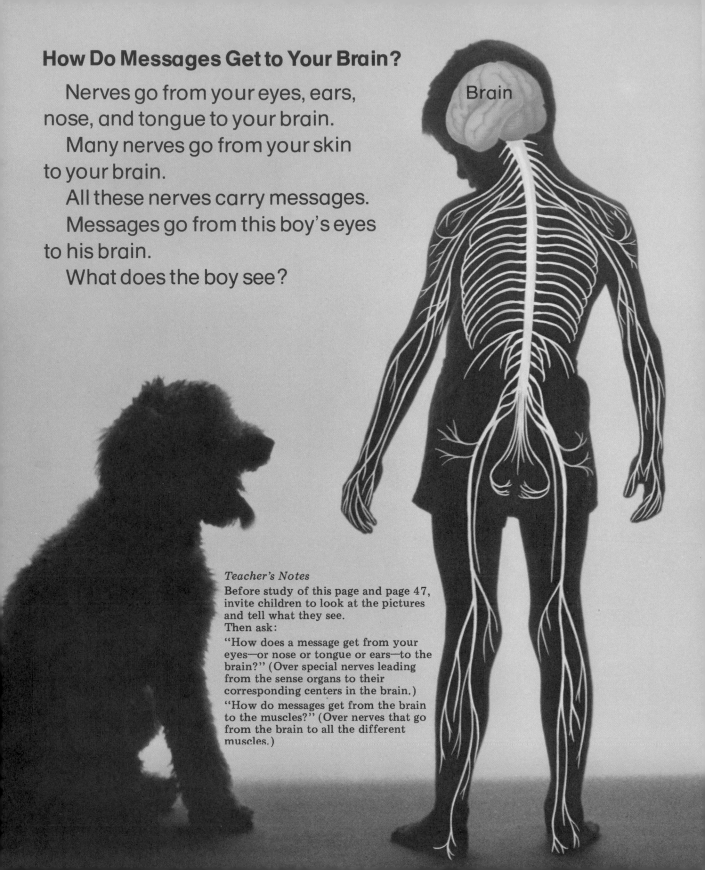

How Do Messages Get to Your Brain?

Nerves go from your eyes, ears, nose, and tongue to your brain.

Many nerves go from your skin to your brain.

All these nerves carry messages.

Messages go from this boy's eyes to his brain.

What does the boy see?

Brain

Teacher's Notes

Before study of this page and page 47, invite children to look at the pictures and tell what they see.

Then ask:

"How does a message get from your eyes—or nose or tongue or ears—to the brain?" (Over special nerves leading from the sense organs to their corresponding centers in the brain.)

"How do messages get from the brain to the muscles?" (Over nerves that go from the brain to all the different muscles.)

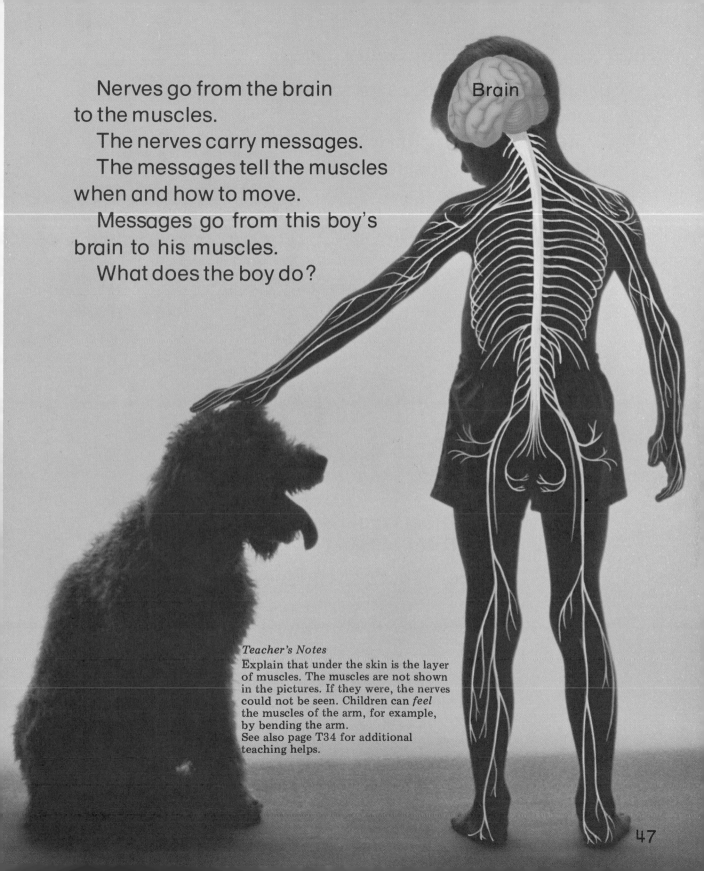

Nerves go from the brain
to the muscles.
The nerves carry messages.
The messages tell the muscles
when and how to move.
Messages go from this boy's
brain to his muscles.
What does the boy do?

Brain

Teacher's Notes
Explain that under the skin is the layer
of muscles. The muscles are not shown
in the pictures. If they were, the nerves
could not be seen. Children can *feel*
the muscles of the arm, for example,
by bending the arm.
See also page T34 for additional
teaching helps.

What Can You Do to Keep Safe?

Your brain gets messages from your senses.

But you must decide what to do.

Each day you must decide how to keep safe.

Read about some safety problems.

Teacher's Notes

An attempt is made here to develop in pupils an attitude of personal responsibility for their own safety. You might ask:

"What did *you* do today to help keep yourself safe?"

To make the safety material more compelling, real-life problems are presented for consideration and decision making.

How Would You Act with a Strange Dog?

Have pupils study the text and the picture on page 49 and suggest tentative answers to the questions. Then have children turn the page to check their ideas.

See also page T34 for additional teaching aids.

How Would You Act with a Strange Dog?

Suppose you see a strange dog.

You hear the dog barking at you.

You don't know what the dog will do.

What will *you* do?

Now turn the page.

The answer: Stand still; talk softly.

If you run, the dog might run after you.

If you shout, you might make the dog angry.

Soon you can try to walk slowly past the dog.

If the dog will not let you go by, walk slowly backward.

Remember: Never tease a dog.

If you tease, the dog may bite.

Here are other safe things to do around dogs.

Why are these things safe to do?

Don't play with a pet while it is eating or drinking.

Don't go into a
yard where there
is a dog unless its
owner is there.

Try not to play
rough games with
a dog. A dog may
bite if it gets excited.

Teacher's Notes
What Should a Bicycle Driver Know?
This lesson begins with a discussion of
hand signals that bicycle drivers should
use, but on page 54 it expands to other
basic bicycle-safety ideas. Note that
here, as in all safety treatments in this
book, only *correct* safety procedures
are shown in pictures. Unsafe actions
are not featured in any of the pictures.

(*Note:* In some communities children
are not permitted to drive bicycles on
the sidewalk. Be sure to check with
the police department in your community to see what the regulations are.)

What Should a Bicycle Driver Know?

Suppose you are on your bicycle.
Soon you plan to make a left turn.
What must you know to make the
turn safely?

Now turn the page.

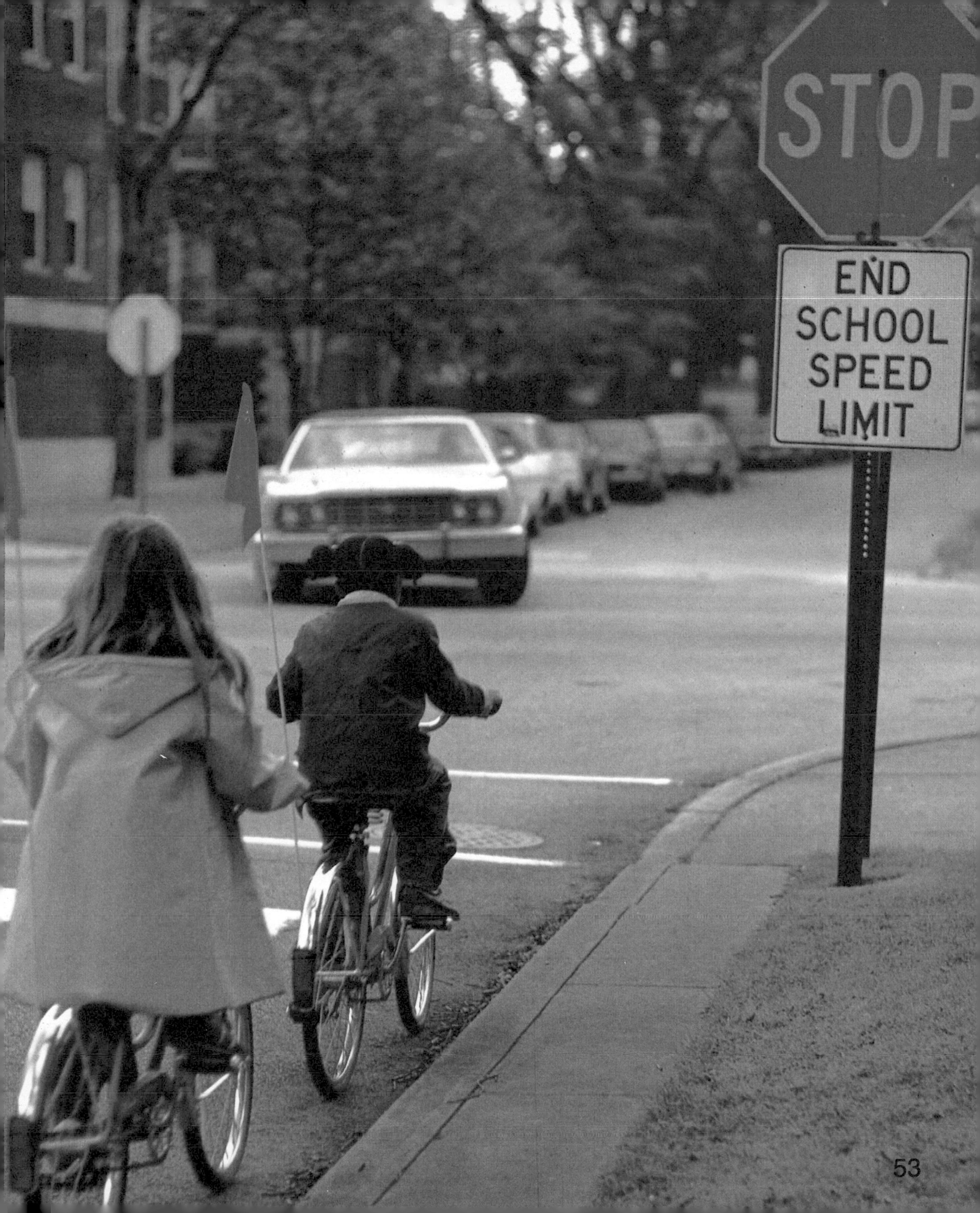
STOP
END
SCHOOL
SPEED
LIMIT

The answer: Know how to signal.

Before you make a right turn, do this.

Before you make a left turn, do this.

Before you stop or slow down, do this.
   Remember: Look before you turn.
Look for people, cars, or bicycles.

   Here are some other bicycle-safety
rules. Why is each rule a good one?

Ride one by one. Do not zigzag.
Ride just one on a bike.

Walk your bike across a busy street.

Have a light and a horn.
Put packages in a basket or carrier.

Teacher's Notes
What If Your Clothes Catch on Fire?
This page and pages 57 and 58 stress
how a child can help himself or herself
if clothing should catch on fire. Other
fire-safety precautions are also noted
on page 58.

What If Your Clothes Catch on Fire?

Suppose you are on a picnic.
You help your father make a fire.
You reach for a new stick.
By mistake you reach across
the fire.
Your clothes catch on fire.
What should you do?

Now turn the page.

56

The answer: Roll on the ground.

You can put a coat or blanket around you too.

This smothers the fire. When you smother the fire, you keep air from it.

There are other things to know about fire safety.

Remember: Put out your campfire.

Light matches only when a grown-up is with you.

Why are these safe things to do?

Teacher's Notes
Encourage re-enactments of what to do if your clothes catch on fire.
Stress, too, what to do if a child should see a fire: *Report it instantly to an adult; do not try to put it out yourself.* See page T35 for additional teaching helps.

Teacher's Notes
The *stop, drop, and roll* technique is now the recommended procedure. It can save lives and often reduces injury caused by clothing fires. Students should practice this technique, if possible, in class (on a clean sheet spread out on the floor) or in the gym on mats. Be sure students know *not to run* if their clothes should catch fire. Running fans the flames.

An excellent fire safety booklet is *All About Fire Safety, Vol. 1,* published by the National Safety Council in 1977. It is for children in kindergarten and early primary grades. Included are teacher's notes and activities on spirit masters. For further information, write the National Safety Council, 425 N. Michigan Ave., Chicago, IL 60611.

JUST LISTEN

Teacher's Notes

Children "just listen" as you read this poem. Later they can read the poem along with you.

Discuss how forest fires get started. Also consider why it is so sad when there are forest fires. (Trees that take years to grow are destroyed; beauty spots are spoiled; animals who live in trees lose their homes and often their lives.)

In a recent year, about two million acres of forest lands burned. So conservation of our forests is a most important topic to consider.

See also page T35 for additional teaching helps.

Forest Fires

Someone built a campfire
  And failed to put it out.
A breeze came up and quickened;
  The embers spread about;
And soon the woods were blazing.
  The fire spread and spread;
The trees that took long years to grow
  Stand blackened now and dead.

A lighted match can
start a forest fire.
  A lighted cigarette can
start a fire too.
  What are safe things
to do?

"Forest Fires" is to be read to children as they just listen.

"Forest Fires" by Myrtle Carpenter from *Poems Children Enjoy.*
Printed with permission of the publisher, The Instructor Publications, Inc., Dansville, New York 14437.

Teacher's Notes
Should You Take Another Person's Medicine?
Some important ideas about safety in connection with medicines (drugs) are developed on pages 60 and 63.

Should You Take Another Person's Medicine?

Suppose you are at your friend's house.

You do not feel well.

Your friend says, "We have some medicine.

"Why don't you take it?

"It will make you feel better."

What will you do?

Now turn the page.

61

The answer: Don't take another person's medicine.

It could make you very sick.
Never take any medicine by yourself.

A grown-up you know should give it to you.

Here you can see some other ideas about safety with medicines.
Why are these safe things to do?

Teacher's Notes

In the course of discussing pages 62 and 63, explain what a drug is. (A drug is something that can make changes in the body. Many drugs are called *medicines*.)

Consider, too, ways in which drugs can be helpful if used *properly*:

Drugs may help pain in the body go away.

Drugs may kill the germs that cause problems such as a sore throat.

Drugs in the shots a doctor gives can keep us from getting certain diseases.

Do not take any pill or liquid.
Go home and tell about it.

Teacher's Notes

Emphasize that a drug that can help can be harmful at times. It can be harmful if it is not used in the right way:

Too much of a drug can make a person sick.

Too much of a drug can make a person dizzy or sleepy or confused.

Too much of a drug can even kill a person.

That is why drugs should only be taken if needed and why they must be used exactly according to directions.

See also page T35 for additional teaching suggestions.

Use medicine just as the doctor says. Or use it just as the directions say.

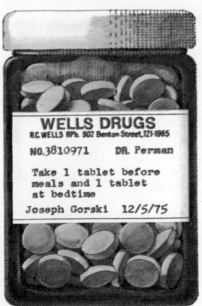

Medicines are not candy. Keep them where little children can't get them.

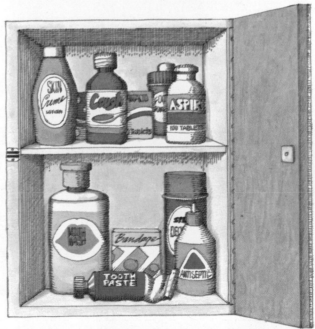

Teacher's Notes
How Can You Be Safe on a Class Trip?
Discuss trips the group has taken and
safety precautions observed on the
trips. Then turn attention to the safety
problem raised in the picture on page 65.

How Can You Be Safe on a Class Trip?

Suppose you take a trip
with your class.

You go in a school bus.

How can you be a safe rider?

What else will you do to keep
safe on the trip?

Now turn the page.

The answer: Follow class safety rules.

Before you go, your class should make safety rules.

Your class might make these:

Stay in your seat on the bus.
Never put arms or head out a window.
Take turns getting on and off the bus.
Do not bother the bus driver.
Stay with the class at all times.
Do not touch any machines.

How do these rules help you?

Teacher's Notes
Talk over "The answer" given here.
Then see if pupils have additional
safety suggestions to offer. (Don't put
books or lunch boxes in the aisle where
others can trip over them; stand on the
curb while waiting for the bus to arrive;
and so on.)
Point out that many safety rules for
trips apply to daily school-bus rides
as well.
See also page T35 for additional
teaching helps.

SAFETY AROUND US

Look around you every day.
You will see safety signs.
You will see safety helpers.
Here are some things you may see.
How does each one help you?

Teacher's Notes

This page is designed to help children become increasingly aware of safety "in action" in the world around them. In discussing this page, ask for demonstrations of what safety-patrol members do when they want children to *stop* at a crossing and when they think it is safe for children to *go*. Children might also describe safety aids they often see. Such safety aids as *crosswalks, safety islands, overpasses,* and *underpasses* might be discussed. See also page T35 for additional teaching ideas.

Activities

Teacher's Notes

Another thing youngsters might do is to make a puppet show—using paper-bag puppets—about safety with medicines. The show might then be given to another group.

See also page T35 for additional teaching aids.

Things to Do

1. Draw a picture that shows a safe way to ride a bicycle.

2. Try to guess this riddle:
   It can help you.
   But it can hurt you.
   You should not get too close to it.
   Its name starts with *f*.
   What is it?

3. See if you can make a rhyme:
   Two on a bicycle must not be.
   Just one rider is the rule for ___.

4. See if you can guess this riddle:
   They help keep you safe.
   You see safety signs with them.
   You have two of them.
   What are they?

Do You Remember?

Teacher's Notes

This page reviews some important safety ideas developed in *Book One*. These ideas still need emphasizing. Stress particularly these points: looking for turning cars before crossing a street when the signal is green, crossing only at corners or on crosswalks, not going off with a stranger and not going off even with a known person without first going home to get permission, and reporting to a teacher (at school) or a grown-up (at home) when one feels sick or has been hurt.
See also page T35 for additional teaching suggestions.

There are other safe things to do.
You may have learned them last year.
Do you remember them?

1. What should you do when a traffic signal looks like this?

2. Where is the safe place to cross a street?

3. What should you do if a stranger asks you to go with him or her?

4. What should you do when a traffic signal looks like this?

5. What should you do if you hurt yourself?

6. What should you do if you do not feel well?

Can You Show What You Know?

1. Tell how your eyes keep you safe.

2. Tell how your ears keep you safe.

3. Tell what you learn from your sense of touch.

4. Show what to do if you meet a strange dog.

5. Show how to give these bicycle signals: left turn, right turn, slow down or stop.

6. Tell why you need your brain.

7. Show what to do if your clothes catch on fire.

8. Tell about some safe ways to take medicine if you need it.

Teacher's Notes
Here behavioral objectives in the cognitive area are posed in childlike language directly to the youngsters themselves. In turn, boys and girls give evidence by *observable behavior* of what they have learned.

Some other hoped-for but not so easily observed behavioral objectives lie chiefly in the affective area—objectives that pertain to feelings, attitudes, and values. Some of them are:

Appreciates how the senses contribute to our safety and to keeping us in touch with the world around us.

Is aware of each person's responsibility for his or her own safety.

Practices the rules of bicycle safety.

Realizes the importance of using medicines, if needed, exactly as directed—and of children not taking medicine on their own.

Is aware of efforts in the community to help safeguard people.

Observes safety precautions around animals.

Recognizes the need to be careful around campfires.

Behavioral objectives in the cognitive area are stated here directly to children themselves.

70

Yes or No?

Teacher's Notes
This "Yes or No?" exercise is a simple test, presented in a form that children enjoy. They look upon it as a form of puzzle.
Have pupils read each question silently and be ready to tell the answer. Or, if children are able, they might write on their papers each number and after it the correct answer, *yes* or *no*. You can also discuss why each child answered as he or she did.
Answers to the questions are:
1. no; 2. yes; 3. no; 4. yes; 5. yes; 6. no; 7. no; 8. no; 9. no.

1. Is it safe to take another person's medicine?

2. Should you roll on the ground if your clothes catch on fire?

3. Is it safe to tease a dog?

4. Should you signal before you make a turn on a bicycle?

5. Should you stay with the class when you go on a trip?

6. Should you play with matches?

7. Should you shout and run about on the school bus?

8. Should two people ride on a bicycle?

9. Is it safe to take a strange pill?

Fill in the Answer
(Do not write in the book.)

Teacher's Notes
This page gives children experience with a fill-in type of test. Have pupils read each item silently and be prepared to write or tell the answer. If children write their answers, let them copy the number of each item and then fill in the missing word. They can find correct spellings by referring to pages in this chapter where the words are used.

1. You think with your br__.

2. You taste with your t__.

3. You smell with your n__.

4. You hear with your e__.

5. You see with your e__.

6. Your sense of touch is in your sk__.

7. Messages go to the brain over n__.

8. The five main senses are
   s__ing
   h__ing
   sm__ing
   ta__ing
   to__ing

SCHOOL & HOME

Teacher's Notes
This page encourages youngsters to share with their families safety ideas learned at school.

Make a stick puppet of YOU.
Practice with your puppet.
Have your puppet tell your family about safety.
What will the puppet say about *bicycles*?
What will the puppet say about *medicines*?

3 About Your Health Questions

What health questions do you have?

Words to Know
bread
cereal
exercise
fruit
meat
milk
sleep
vegetables

Teacher's Notes
See the Enrichment Suggestions for Chapter Three on pages T36–T38. See also the suggested Reference Materials on pages T44–T45.

Vocabulary Development Introduce the **Words to Know**: *sleep, exercise, milk, fruit, vegetables, meat, cereal, bread.* Other words used in Chapter 3 are *bones, breakfast, dental hygienist, dentist, doctor, energy, food, grow, healthy, joints, muscles, nurse, permanent, primary, six-year molars, skeleton, teeth, toilet, wash.*

75

How Will You Find Answers To Your Health Questions?

You may have questions about how you grow.

You may have questions about food or sleep or exercise.

Here is one way to find answers to your questions.

How else can you find answers?

Teacher's Notes

Discuss information sources for the health questions children have: parents, the school nurse (shown on these pages), the teacher, books of information.

After you read the poem on page 77 to pupils, talk it over with them. Discuss the values of being curious and of asking questions about things. Life is more interesting when we keep thinking of things we want to know about. Also, thinking of the "why" of things and then seeking answers is how we learn effectively.

See also page T36 for additional teaching aids.

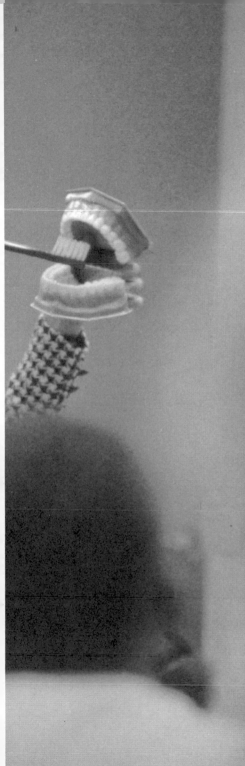

JUST LISTEN

Tell Me

And *why* do I have to go to bed?
And why can't children fly?
Or tell me, for a change, instead:
WHY
Do I ask Why?

What "why" questions do you have?

"Tell Me" from *All Together* by Dorothy Aldis. Copyright 1925, 1926, 1927, 1928, 1934, 1939, 1952 by Dorothy Aldis. Reprinted by permission of G.P. Putnam's Sons.

Why Aren't Children the Same Age the Same Size?

Each of you is different.

Each of you has a different way of growing.

That is how it will be all the years you are growing.

You will grow *your* way.

Others your age will grow their way.

Look at others your age.

Are some taller than you?

Are some shorter than you?

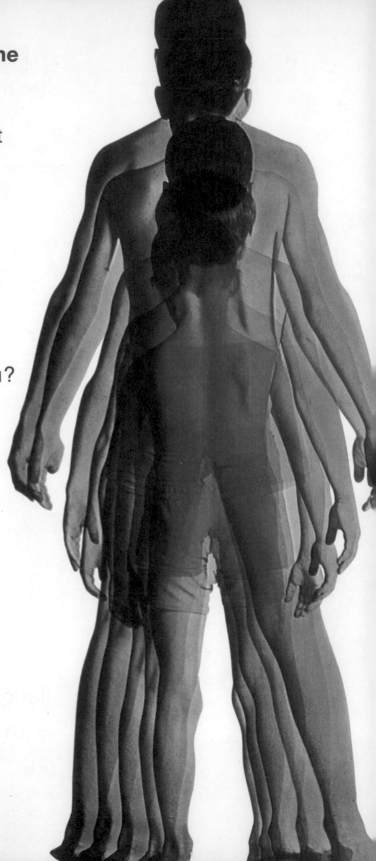

Teacher's Notes

Explore children's ideas about the answer to the often-asked question posed in the title.

Then have youngsters study the page. Later ask:

"What have you learned about how children grow?"

"Now how would you answer the question, 'Why?'"

"Is *size* the most important thing about a person?" (No, the important thing is what kind of person she or he is. We don't pick our friends, for example, because they are tall or short. We pick them because they are likable or friendly or thoughtful, and so on.)

To dramatize the fact that differences in height and weight and body build are natural and to be expected among children the same age, let volunteers form a line in front of the room. The differences will be apparent.

See also page T36 for other teaching helps.

What Kinds of Foods Should You Eat?

You need different kinds of foods each day.

The foods help you grow. They give you energy. They keep you healthy.

One or *two* kinds of foods cannot do all these things.

You need foods from each food group.

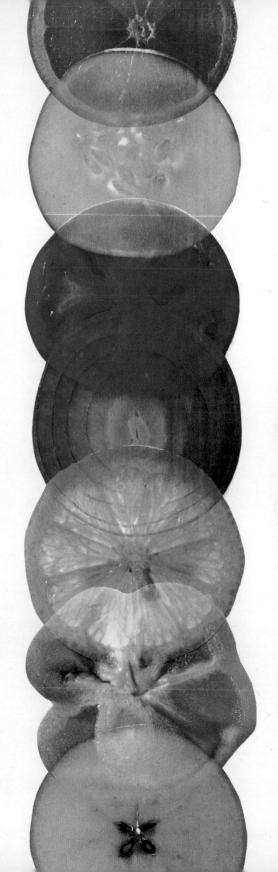

Teacher's Notes

Review what food does for us as set forth in *Book One*. (Food gives us energy for work and play, helps us keep healthy, helps us grow; lack of proper food can make us feel tired.) Encourage preliminary discussion about why we need a variety of foods. Then let pupils study the page to check on their ideas.

Ask these questions:

"Why *do* we need different kinds of foods?" (Be sure pupils understand that a person can eat the same foods for several days—as long as the person gets enough of each food from the different food groups each day.)

"What do the different foods, working together, do for you?"

Remind children that eating the right food helps promote healthy teeth and gums too.

See also page T37.

What Are Some Foods in the Milk Group?

You need *two or three cups* of milk each day.

How can you get some milk without drinking it? Many foods are made *from* milk or *with* milk.

What foods do you like that are made from or with milk?

What Are Some Foods in the Vegetables and Fruits Group?

What fruits do you like to eat?

What vegetables do you like to eat?

What green vegetables can you name?

What yellow vegetables can you name?

Try to eat *four or more servings*

of vegetables and fruits every day.

You can eat them at meals.

You can eat them for snacks.

Teacher's Notes

Give children an opportunity to name as many of the pictured foods as they can. Foods included in the picture are: carrots, orange, grapefruit, sweet potato, strawberries, broccoli, peach, apple, pear, cabbage, cantaloupe, squash, green pepper, tomato, acorn squash, papaya, turnip, lemon, pumpkin, grapes. Then ask them to name other green and yellow vegetables they may know. Broaden the discussion to include talk about fruits children like especially. Why do they like a given fruit? Is it the color? The taste? The smell? The crunching sound made when chewing it? Or what? Do the same thing in exploring the kinds of vegetables pupils particularly like.

What Are Some Foods in the Meat Group?

Some foods in the Meat Group are not *meat.*

Which ones are they?

Try to eat *two servings* from the meat group every day.

Have you had some of these foods today?

Teacher's Notes

Encourage pupils to name the various foods shown here. Foods included in the picture are: ham, eggs, liver, fish, peanut butter, ground beef, chicken, hot dogs, lentils, pork chop, lamb roast, sausage, beef roast, bacon. Other foods in the alternate group— not shown—are dry beans, dry peas, nuts.

What Are Some Foods in the Breads and Cereals Group?

What hot cereals do you like?

What cold cereals do you like?

What kinds of bread can you name?

Try to eat *four or more servings* from the breads and cereals group every day.

What breads and cereals have you had today?

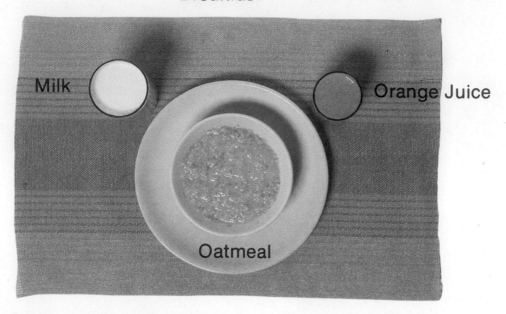

Breakfast

Milk

Orange Juice

Oatmeal

How Can You Eat Well?

Here is what one girl had one day for breakfast, lunch, and supper.

What foods are from each of these groups?

Vegetables and Fruits Group
Meat Group
Milk Group
Breads and Cereals Group

Did the girl eat some foods from each food group?

How many servings did she have from each group?

The meals on these pages include foods from all four basic food groups. The meals also reflect the recent recommendations of the U.S. Senate Select Committee on Nutrition and Human Needs. The Committee suggests increased servings of fresh fruit and vegetables, whole-grain bread, and cooked cereal. It suggests a reduction of sweets such as cakes, candy, and sugared soft drinks.
Ask students what they usually eat for a snack. Suggest nutritious snacks that students might try: cheese and crackers; celery with peanut butter; raw vegetables such as carrot sticks, green pepper slices, cucumber slices, pieces of cauliflower; fresh fruit; nuts; bread and butter or bread and peanut butter; cottage cheese; yogurt. If possible, you might introduce some of the snacks at school—such as raw vegetable slices with a simple sour cream or yogurt dip.

Lunch

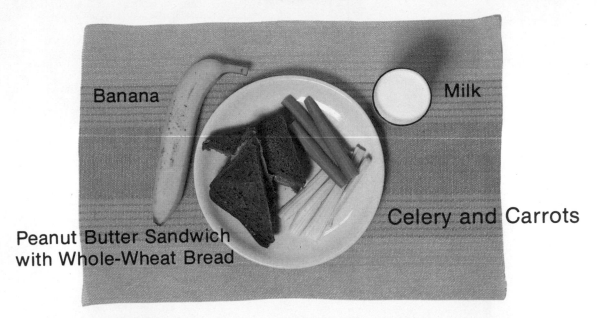

Banana

Milk

Peanut Butter Sandwich
with Whole-Wheat Bread

Celery and Carrots

Supper

Pear

Milk

Macaroni and Cheese

Salad

Vegetable Soup

85

Do Different Families Eat Different Foods?

Each day most families eat foods from the breads and cereals group.

But different families may eat different things.

Here are some foods they may eat for breakfast.

What are they?

Teacher's Notes

Youngsters should know that there are many ways to get an adequate daily diet. Different families have different food preferences and may have widely differing menus. But each family may be getting enough of the right kinds of foods each day. We can't evaluate anyone's daily diet until *all* the foods eaten in meals and in snacks have been noted.

Pages 86 and 87 will help to break down stereotypes some children may have about what is a "good" breakfast. Actually, there are many, many kinds of adequate breakfasts. Other meals, too, may vary from family to family but may be equally nutritious.

Hot Oatmeal

Spaghetti

Grits

Families have other foods
for breakfast too.
What other foods does your
family have?

Teacher's Notes
Ask children if they ever stay overnight
at a friend's home. If so, you might
comment that one of the things that
makes such stays fun is that you may
have a chance to try different foods
for supper and for breakfast. Point out,
too, that a polite guest does not say,
"What is that?" or "I don't want that."
or "I don't think I'll like that." Instead,
the courteous guest tries a little of a
new food without comments. Usually
the guest finds he or she likes it!
See also page T37.

Bagels and Cream Cheese

Rice Pudding with Raisins

Peanut Butter on Toast

Cornbread

Cold Cereal

87

Why Do You Need Sleep?

Sleep helps you feel good.

Sleep helps you grow.

You may feel cross when you do not get enough sleep.

You may make mistakes at school.

Most children your age need about eleven hours of sleep at night.

Some need more than this.

Some need less.

How do you feel when you do not get enough sleep?

Teacher's Notes

See how many reasons children can give for why we need to get enough sleep at night. Then let them check their ideas with the information on this page.

Later, volunteers might act out how a person who has not had enough sleep might look and walk and behave. Ask:

"How can getting enough sleep help you at school?"

See also page T37.

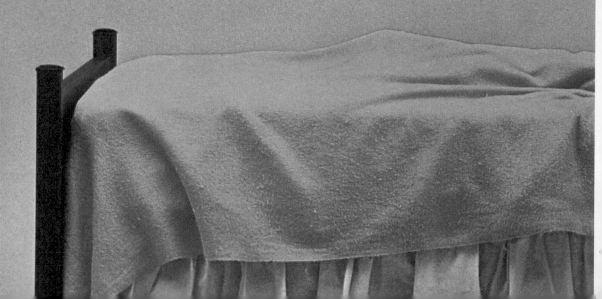

JUST LISTEN

Teacher's Notes

Children "just listen" as you read this poem to them. Later they can read it along with you.

Point out that when we sleep our brain is never completely at rest. During our waking hours, the brain helps us pay attention to what we see, hear, touch, taste, smell. At night, although the body rests during sleep, the brain is still active.

See also page T37.

Children of this age may occasionally be troubled by bad dreams. You might mention that it is normal to have scary dreams, and that almost everyone has them at some time. Let individuals tell about their bad dreams if they want to.

All Asleep

My eyes can see,
My feet can walk,
My ears can hear,
My mouth can talk.

My nose can smell,
My tongue can lick,
My teeth can bite,
My toes can kick.

But while I sleep
The whole night through,
They all are still—
They're sleeping, too!

Do you move a little
in your sleep?
How do you know?

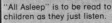

Why Do You Need Exercise?

Exercise helps keep you healthy.
Exercise can help build strong muscles.

Exercise can be fun too.

Maybe you like to play tag.

Maybe you like to skate or play ball or swim.

In these and other ways you can have fun.

How do *you* like to get exercise?

Teacher's Notes

Explore children's ideas about why they need exercise. Then let them check their ideas with the information on this page.
Ask:

"What do you think keeps some boys and girls from getting enough exercise?" (They may sit for too many hours watching TV instead of playing outdoors.)

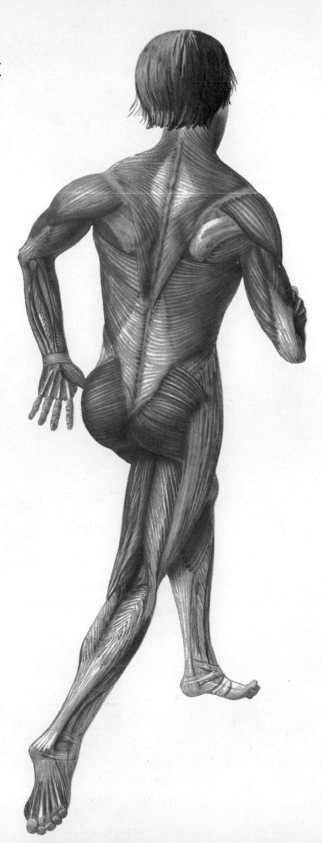

Why Can You Move As You Do?

Do you know why you can bend and twist and turn?

Your skeleton has bending places in it. These bending places are called *joints*.

Why can you bend your fingers?

You can move your arms because you have joints. The joints are at your shoulders and your elbows.

Where are some joints in your legs?

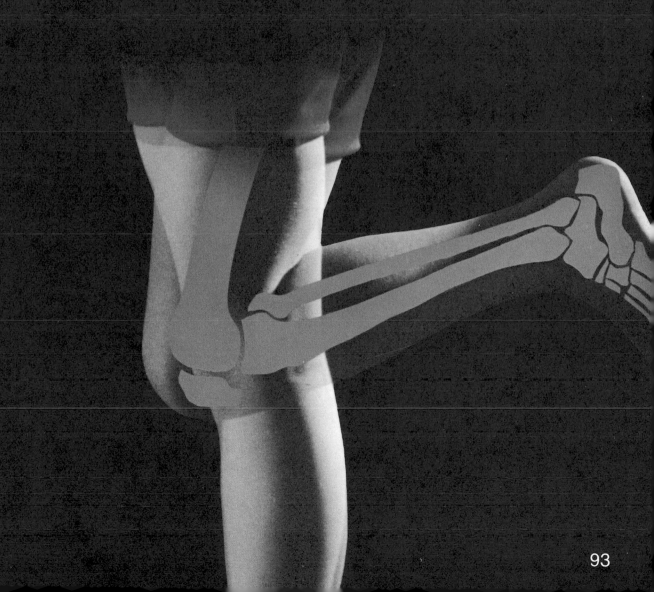

There are many joints in your backbone.
Each bone is set one on top of the other.
They move when you bend.

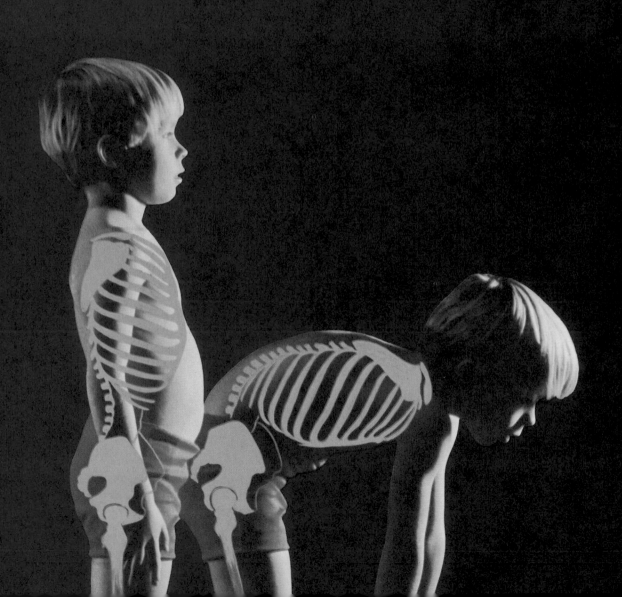

The small bones move when you
twist too.
Put your hand on your backbone.
Can you feel the small bones
in your back move?

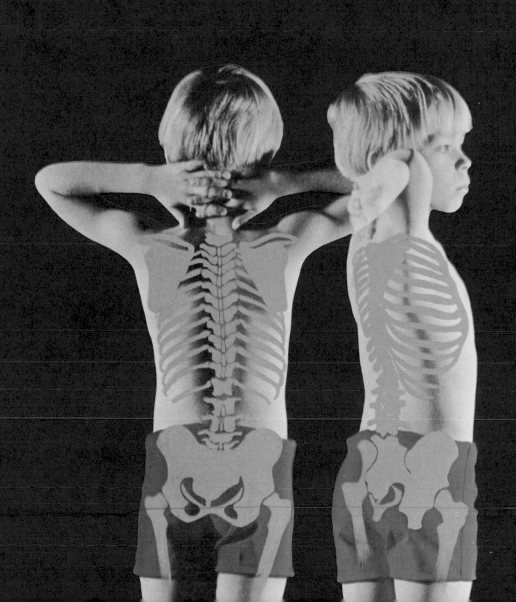

JUST LOOK

This painting was made long ago.
The children played then much
as they do now.
How are they playing?
How do you like to play?

Pieter Brueghel: *Children's Games*,
Kunsthistorisches Museum, Vienna.

Why Should You Wash Your Hands?

Most of the time your hands look clean.

But there are germs on them. Germs can make you sick. You cannot see germs. They are too tiny.

Wash your hands before you eat. Then you wash away germs.

Wash your hands after you use the toilet too.

How does this help you stay well?

Teacher's Notes
In connection with pages 98 and 99, you might explain that all around us are plants so tiny you cannot see them without a microscope. These little plants are called *bacteria*. Many bacteria help us, but others can make us sick. We call the ones that make us sick *disease germs*.
Let children study the page to find out *when* the hands should be washed. Mention that the best way to wash the hands is to use warm water and soap. Other times to wash the hands are before preparing or serving food, after blowing the nose, after using hands or handkerchief to cover a cough or sneeze, and after handling animals. See also page T37.

99

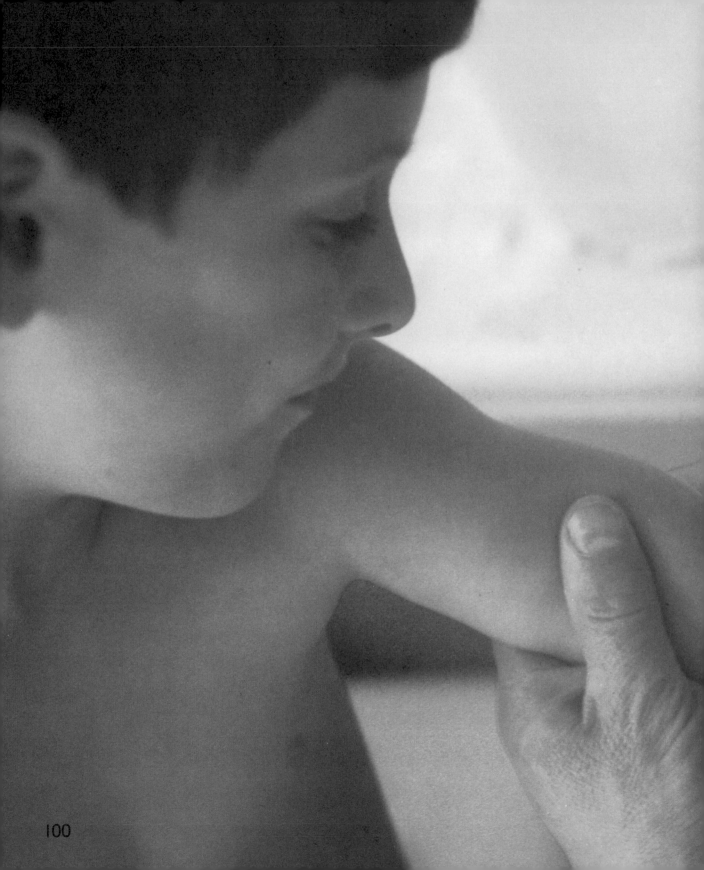

Teacher's Notes
Review with pupils the things they learned in *Book One* about what a doctor does in a health checkup. The doctor, or the nurse, may take the temperature, check the pulse at the wrist, check the eyes, give any necessary shots (or give a lump of sugar or some syrup with medicine in it that keeps us from getting the disease called polio). The doctor listens to the heart and lungs with a stethoscope, looks into the ears and nose and mouth, feels the "insides" of the body, checks posture. If any medicines are needed, the doctor writes out a prescription for them. The prescription is taken to a drugstore where the pharmacist fills it.
(*Note:* In many parts of the country nurse practitioners are now doing these physical assessments.)

Why Should You Go to the Doctor When You're Not Sick?

Sometimes you need a health checkup.

The doctor gives it to you.

A nurse may help the doctor.

The doctor can tell you how to stay well.

Sometimes you need a shot.

The doctor or nurse can give it to you.

How can a shot help you?

How Should You Watch TV?

Sit well back from the TV set.

Have a light on by the TV set when you watch TV at night.

Don't watch TV hour after hour.

Look away from the TV now and then. This will rest your eyes.

Some people on TV want you to buy things.

Don't expect people in your family to buy everything.

Families must think before they buy.

What will they think about?

When Do Your New Teeth Come In?

Each boy and girl is different.

Some children are five when they lose their first teeth. Some children are six.

Some may be seven before this happens.

When it is right for you, you will lose your first teeth, or *primary teeth*.

Then *permanent teeth* will take their places.

Permanent teeth are growing in your jaw right now. In time, you will have 32 permanent teeth.

No other teeth will form under them. They are the last teeth you will get. That is why they are called permanent teeth.

This girl has some permanent teeth. Why should she take care of them?

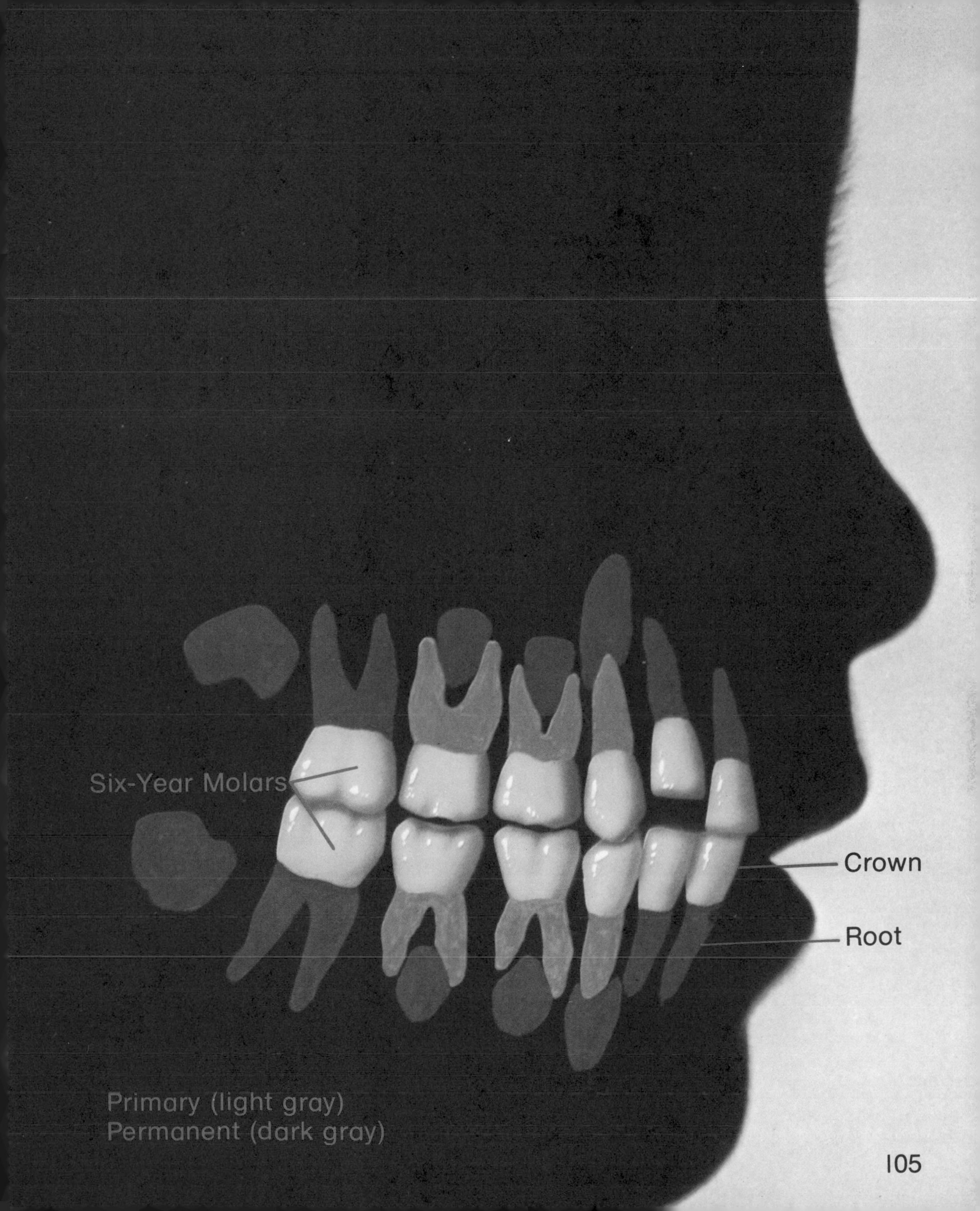

Six-Year Molars

Crown

Root

Primary (light gray)
Permanent (dark gray)

How Should You Take Care of Your Teeth?

Floss your teeth. Your teacher or the school nurse will show you how. The dentist or the dental hygienist can show you too.

If you can, brush your teeth after you eat.

If you can't do this, brush them well at least once a day.

Brush back and forth, back and forth.

How will brushing help?

If you can, go to a *dentist* for checkups. If you have a cavity, the dentist will fill it.

Teacher's Notes
The suggestions for tooth care on this page and the next one include the latest recommendations of the American Dental Association and the National Institutes of Health, Division of Dental Health, National Institute of Dental Research.
The procedures suggested are thought to be most effective in removing *plaque* from the teeth. *Plaque* is a sticky, colorless film of bacteria that constantly forms on the teeth, especially around the gum line. If plaque is not removed, it builds up and gets beneath the gum line. Eventually it hardens into tartar (which dentists call calculus). This tartar offers still more places for plaque to collect and further attack teeth and gums.

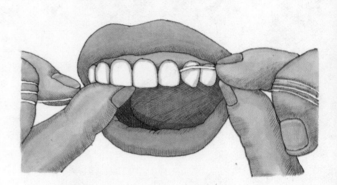

Floss your teeth.

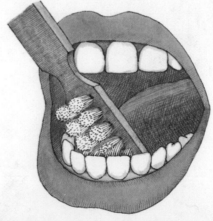

Brush up and down on the insides of the front teeth.

Teacher's Notes
Flossing is essential for removing the plaque that the toothbrush cannot reach. If the school nurse is not available to demonstrate flossing, you can do it. Gently slide the floss between the teeth with a "sawing" motion. Do not snap the floss against the gums. Move the floss away from the gums by scraping the floss up and down against the side of a tooth. Guide the children in practicing the short back-and-forth "scrubbing" strokes with a "pretend" toothbrush. Mention that in a dental health checkup, the *dentist* or the *dental hygienist* will clean the teeth in a special way.
See also page T38.

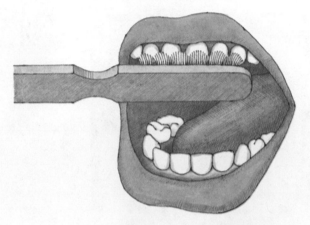

Brush the uppers.

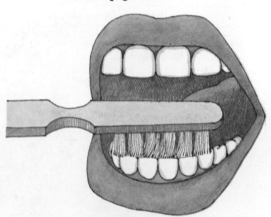

Brush the tops.

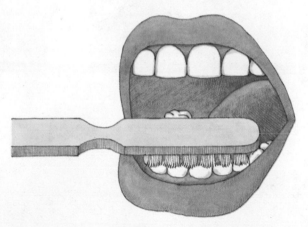

Brush the lowers.

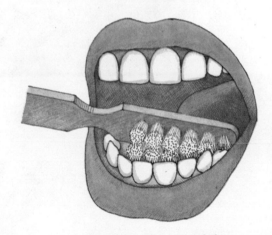

Brush the insides.

HEALTH AROUND US

There is someone in your neighborhood who helps when medicine is needed.

This person works in a drugstore.

This person gets ready the medicine a doctor has ordered.

What is this person called?

Do You Remember?

Teacher's Notes
This page reviews some health
ideas that were first presented
in *Book One* of this series.
The answers:

1. Stay home and get lots of
rest. By so doing, you may
help yourself get over the
cold, and you will also keep
from spreading cold germs
to others.

2. Cover your cough or
sneeze, preferably with a
tissue.

3. Wear rubbers or boots;
carry an umbrella or wear
a raincoat and hat.

4. Answers will vary; cold
cereal, an orange or apple
or banana, and a glass of
milk are possible responses.

5. To keep you from
getting a certain disease
or diseases.

6. To chew food.

7. Tell your teacher or your
parent or whoever is in
charge of you.

8. A grown-up who knows
the kind of medicine you
need.

See also page T38.

There are other healthful things to do.
You may have learned them last year.
Do you remember them?

1. What is a good thing to do when you
have a cold?

2. What should you do when you cough
or sneeze?

3. What should you wear on a rainy day?

4. What could you fix for breakfast
without doing any cooking?

5. Why does the doctor or the nurse give
you a shot?

6. Why do you need your teeth?

7. What should you do if you hurt yourself?

8. Who should give you medicine at home?

Activities

Teacher's Notes
Youngsters who are curious to learn more about germs might look for the book *The True Book of Bacteria* by Anne Frahm (Childrens Press). This book is easy enough for many seven-year-olds to read. Later, reports can be presented to the group.
See also page T38.

Things To Do

1. Draw a picture of a food that smells good when it is cooking.

2. Make up a riddle about a food you like.

3. Complete the sentences below.
    Six foods I like to eat are...
    Five active games I like to play are..
    Four quiet games I like to play are..
    Three ways I help my family are...
    Two records I like to listen to are.
    One food I can fix by myself is...

4. Play the game "Fox and Geese."
    One player is *It*.
    Other players make a line.
    It will try to catch the player
    at the end of the line.
    What will the first one in line
    try to do?

Can You Show What You Know?

1. Tell why you do not grow in the very same way a friend your age does.

2. Draw a food from each food group.

3. Draw a picture that shows how you feel if you do not get enough sleep.

4. Tell how exercise helps you.

5. Tell why you can bend and twist and turn.

6. Tell when you should wash your hands.

7. Show how to brush your teeth.

8. Tell why you should go to a doctor for health checkups.

9. Tell how a dentist can help you.

10. Draw a good thing to do when you watch TV.

Teacher's Notes

Here behavioral objectives in the cognitive area are posed in childlike language directly to the children themselves. In turn, boys and girls give evidence by *observable behavior* of what they have learned.

Other hoped-for objectives lie chiefly in the affective area which is less easily observed. Such objectives pertain to feelings, attitudes, and values. Some of them are:

Is aware of individual differences in growth.

Asks questions about health and does some independent research to find answers.

Enjoys some health-related poems.

Is willing to try different foods and tries to eat enough from the basic four food groups each day.

Realizes that families vary in food patterns and preferences.

Realizes the need for getting enough sleep.

Shows interest in outdoor games and in getting exercise daily.

Enjoys a work of art.

Initiates such healthful practices as washing the hands before eating and after using the toilet.

Is aware of the purpose of health checkups.

Is sensitive to the purposes of advertisements on television.

Engages in good TV-viewing practices.

Assumes responsibility for brushing the teeth.

See also page T38.

Behavioral objectives in the cognitive area are stated here directly to children themselves.

Yes or No?

Teacher's Notes

This "Yes or No?" exercise is a simple test. Have pupils read each question silently and be ready to tell the answer. Or, if children are able, they might write on their papers each number and after it the correct answer, *yes* or *no*. You might then discuss the reasons for each answer given.

Answers to the questions are:
1. yes; 2. yes; 3. yes; 4. yes; 5. no;
6. no; 7. yes; 8. yes; 9. no; 10. yes.

1. Do foods help you grow?

2. Should you try to eat different kinds of foods each day?

3. Should you wash your hands before you eat?

4. Do you need about eleven hours of sleep each night?

5. Do you grow in the very same way your friends do?

6. Should you watch TV hour after hour?

7. Does exercise help you keep healthy?

8. Does your skeleton have bending places?

9. Should you see a doctor only when you are sick?

10. Should you brush your teeth every day?

SCHOOL & HOME

Teacher's Notes
This page is designed to foster school-home communication. You might go over the contents of the page with pupils and have them act out what they plan to tell and show their parents. See also page T38.

Would you like to surprise your family?
Here are some things you could do at home.
Tell your family about the food groups.
Show the right way to brush the teeth.
Go to bed tonight without being told.
Get up early and help get breakfast.

4 About the Hospital

Have you been in a hospital?
What is it like in a hospital?
How can the people in a hospital help us?

Teacher's Notes
See the Enrichment Suggestions for Chapter Four on pages T39–T40. See also the Reference Materials on page T45.

Vocabulary Development Introduce the **Words to Know**: *hospital, emergency room, bones, operating room, cast.* Other words used in Chapter 4 are *animal, blood, emergency, laboratory, operating, pulse, recovery, temperature, X-ray picture.*

Words to Know
bones
cast
emergency room
hospital
operating room

What Happened to Bobby?

Bobby fell from a tree one day.
Mother thought his leg was broken.
Daddy carried Bobby to the car.
Mother and Daddy took Bobby to the hospital.

Bobby felt a little scared.
At the hospital Bobby was put on a hospital cart.

Then Bobby was taken to the *emergency room.*

What will happen there?

Teacher's Notes

Explain that Bobby was taken to the hospital because hospitals are places where doctors and nurses are specially trained to help those who are sick or hurt, and that hospitals have many things to help us get well which are not available at home. You might also point out that many babies are born in hospitals.

Call attention to the blanket wrapped around Bobby's leg. His father put it there to keep his leg straight and comfortable until the doctor could examine it. Mention, too, that a person being cared for at a hospital is called a *patient.*

Explain that the emergency room is the first place that an accident patient is examined.

See also page T39.

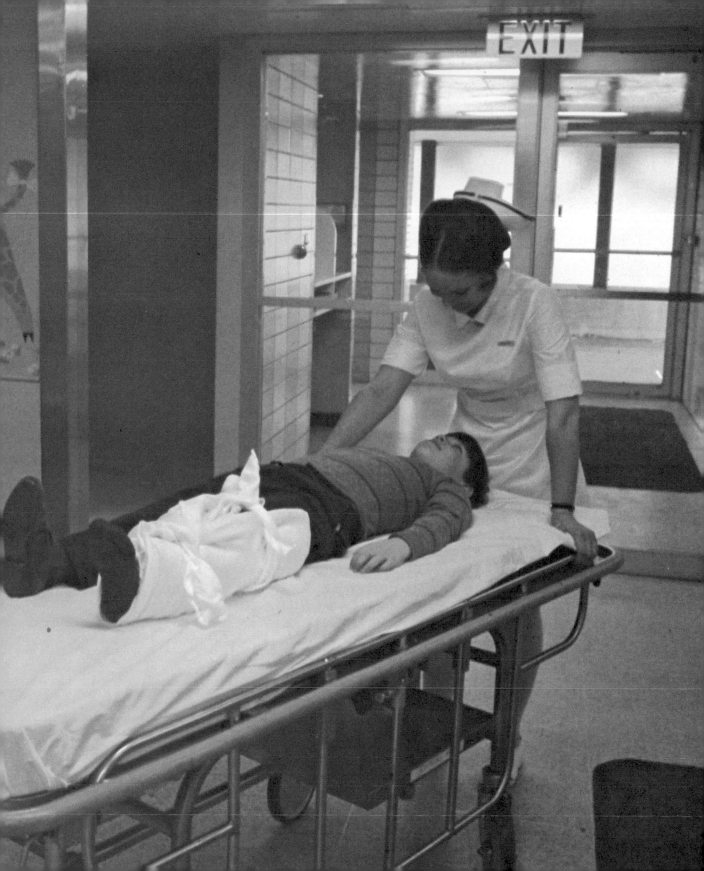

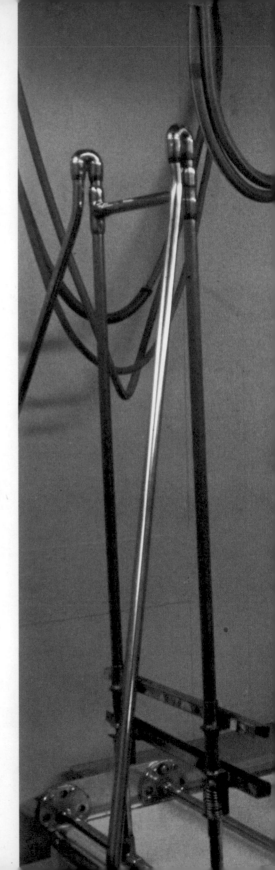

What Is an X-Ray Picture?

An intern came to help Bobby.

Interns are doctors who are learning as they work.

The intern looked at Bobby's leg.

"Off you go again, Bobby," he said.

"Off you go to the *X-ray room.*"

Bobby's cart was pushed to the X-ray room.

An X-ray picture was taken.

It showed the bones in Bobby's leg.

What had happened to the bones?

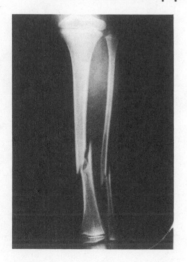

Teacher's Notes

Explain that small hospitals may not have interns.

After children have read the page, ask:

"What is an X-ray picture?"

"What does the X-ray picture on this page show?"

"What else besides bones can an X-ray picture show?" (Organs inside us such as the stomach, heart, and lungs; also X-ray pictures can show the insides of the teeth.)

See also page T39.

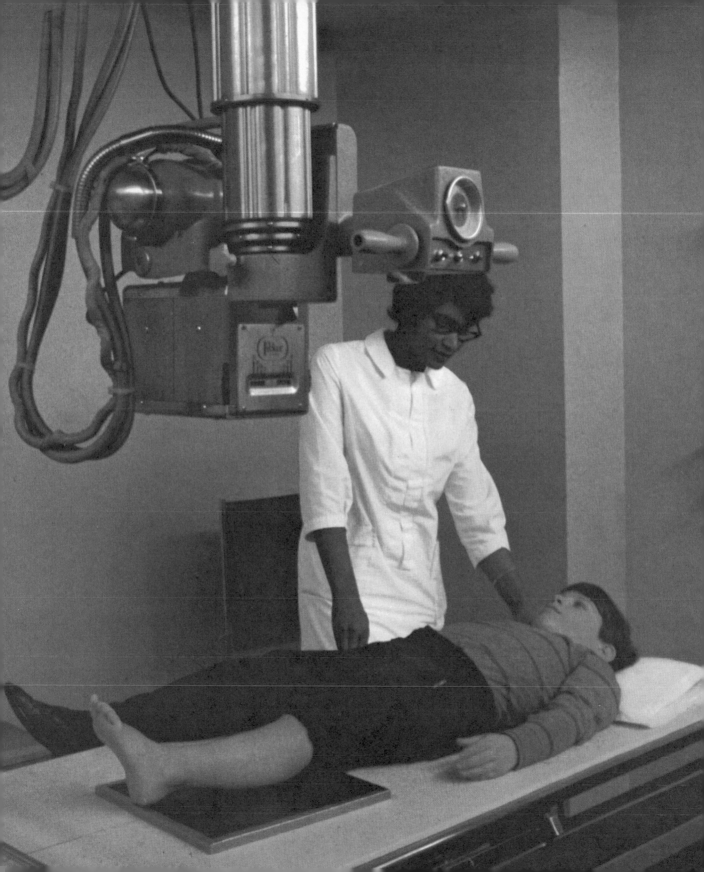

What Did the Doctor Say?

Bobby was taken back to the emergency room.

Soon Dr. Zack came in.

He had seen the X-ray picture.

He told Bobby his leg bones were broken.

"Pretty soon you will go to the *operating room,*" said Dr. Zack.

"We will help you go to sleep.

"Then we will *set* your leg.

"We will put it in a *cast.*

"The cast will keep the broken bones in place.

"This helps the broken bones mend.

"We will keep you here at the hospital for a few days."

How will Bobby feel about that?

Teacher's Notes

Explain in detail what is meant by "set your leg." When the doctor sets the leg, he or she puts the broken ends of the bone together. The *cast* is a stiff, heavy bandage that will keep the leg straight while the broken bone mends.
See also page T39.

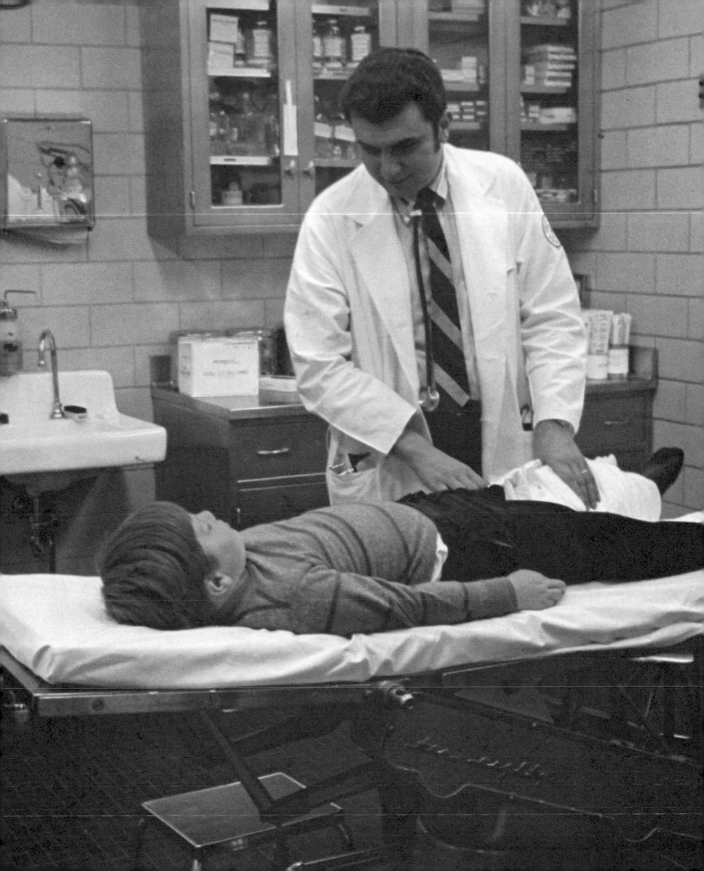

What Is a Hospital Gown?

Bobby did not go to his room yet.
He stayed on the cart.
A nurse gave him a hospital gown.
"A hospital gown opens at the back,"
the nurse said.
"It is easy to get on and off."
Bobby would rather wear his
own pajamas.
Why does he wear a gown instead?

Who Helps at the Hospital?

Soon another nurse came to take Bobby's temperature.

She felt his pulse too.

Then a laboratory worker came.

He took some blood from the tip of Bobby's finger. That hurt a little.

The blood was for some blood tests.

Before long the nurse came back. She said that Dr. Zack was ready.

"Bobby," said the nurse, "when Dr. Zack is through, we will take you to your room."

Who will be waiting for Bobby?

Teacher's Notes

See if youngsters know why the nurse took Bobby's temperature. (To see if it was normal. A normal temperature indicates a lack of infection in the body.)
Ask, too:
"What does it mean to feel the pulse?" (To check the heartbeat as felt in the blood vessels of the wrist. Boys and girls might try to feel their own pulse by putting several fingers from the right hand on the inside wrist of the left hand.)
See also page T40.

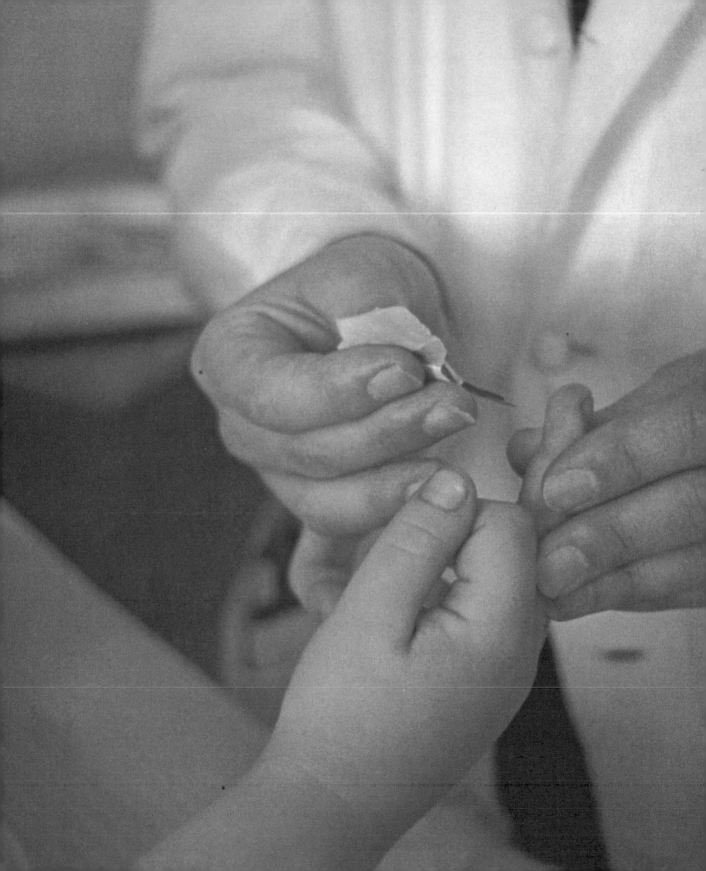

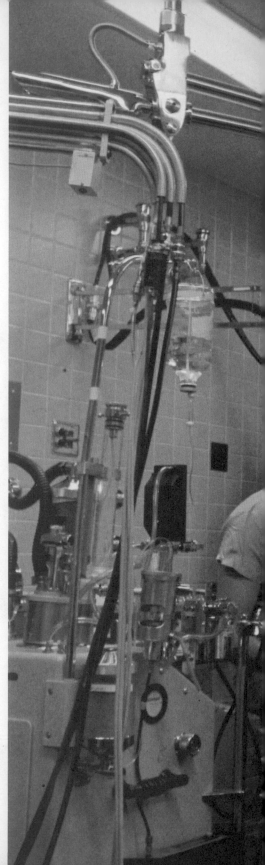

What Happened in the Operating Room?

Away went Bobby on his cart.
He went to the operating room.
"This is Bobby," said Dr. Zack.
A man by a big machine put something over Bobby's nose and mouth.

"Breathe in and out," the man said. "Soon you will be asleep.

"You won't feel a thing."
Soon Bobby *was* asleep.
While Bobby was asleep, Dr. Zack set the broken leg.
Then what did he put on the leg?

Teacher's Notes

Call attention to the masks and caps
the nurses and doctors in the operating
room are wearing. See if children know
why they are worn. (The masks and
the caps help keep the air in the
operating room free of germs.)
Ask:

"Who is the man by the big machine?"
(The *anesthetist*, the person who
helped Bobby go to sleep.)

Point out that Bobby breathed gas
from the machine. This gas is a kind
of drug that causes deep sleep during
which pain cannot be felt.
See also page T40.

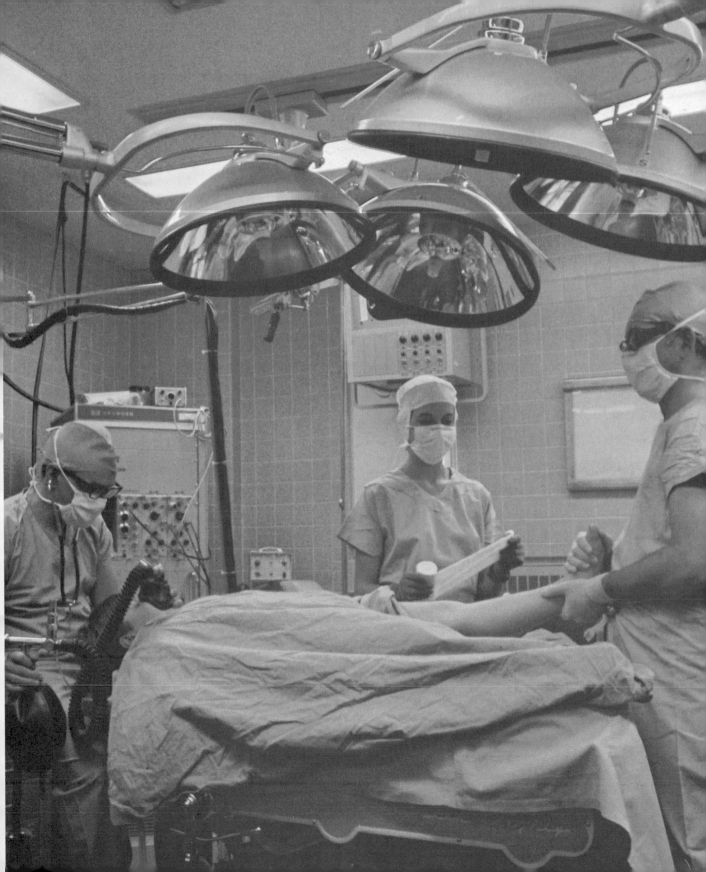

What Happened in Bobby's Room?

When Bobby woke up, he was in the *recovery room.*

But soon a nurse took him to a bed in his new room.

Other boys were there too.

So were Bobby's mother and father.

They looked at Bobby's big cast.

Bobby said he did not feel very well.

The nurse gave him medicine to make him feel better.

Then the nurse said, "I must go. If you need me, push this button."

Later, Bobby's mother and father had to go home. They will be back the next day, won't they?

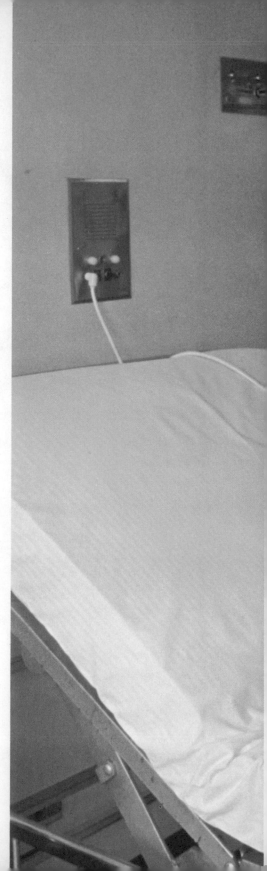

Teacher's Notes

Help youngsters with the term *recovery room,* the room where people stay for a little while after an operation. Explain that Bobby's big cast was what is known as a *walking cast.* The cast kept him from moving his leg. But in a few days he would be able to walk with the cast. The cast had a rubber heel to make walking with it easier. Point out also that Bobby had a special knitted toe-sock; it would help keep his toes warm.
See page T40.

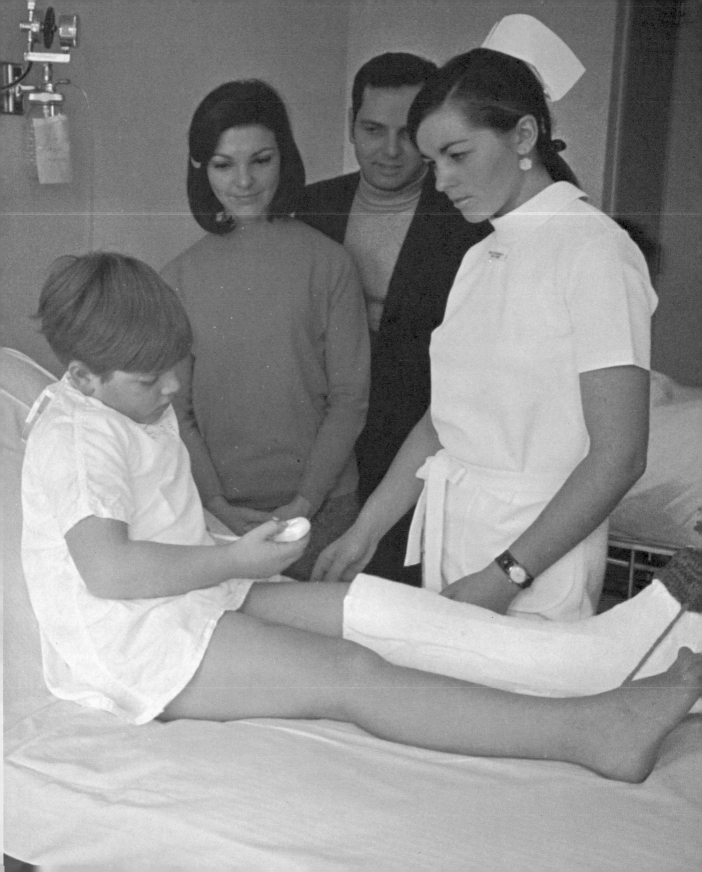

What Happened the Next Morning?

The next morning Bobby felt a little lonely.

But then he made friends with Ben and Pat.

Bobby wanted to walk around. But he had to stay in bed for a day or so.

So he learned about toilet containers for people who must stay in bed.

The nurse helped Bobby wash himself in bed.

She said, "Don't forget to comb your hair. And here is a clean gown."

Later, a worker brought Bobby's breakfast on a tray. It looked good.

What did Bobby do after eating?

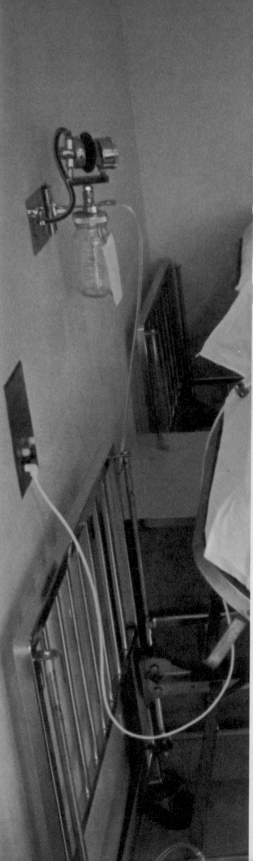

Teacher's Notes

Ask these questions:

"How does a patient go to the toilet at the hospital if he or she cannot get out of bed?" (A bedpan is used; for boys and men, there are also urinals.)

"What are some things Bobby could do for himself at the hospital?" (Wash, comb his hair, put on a clean gown, feed himself, brush his teeth.)

"Where did Bobby eat?" (The tray was brought to him in bed.)

See also page T40.

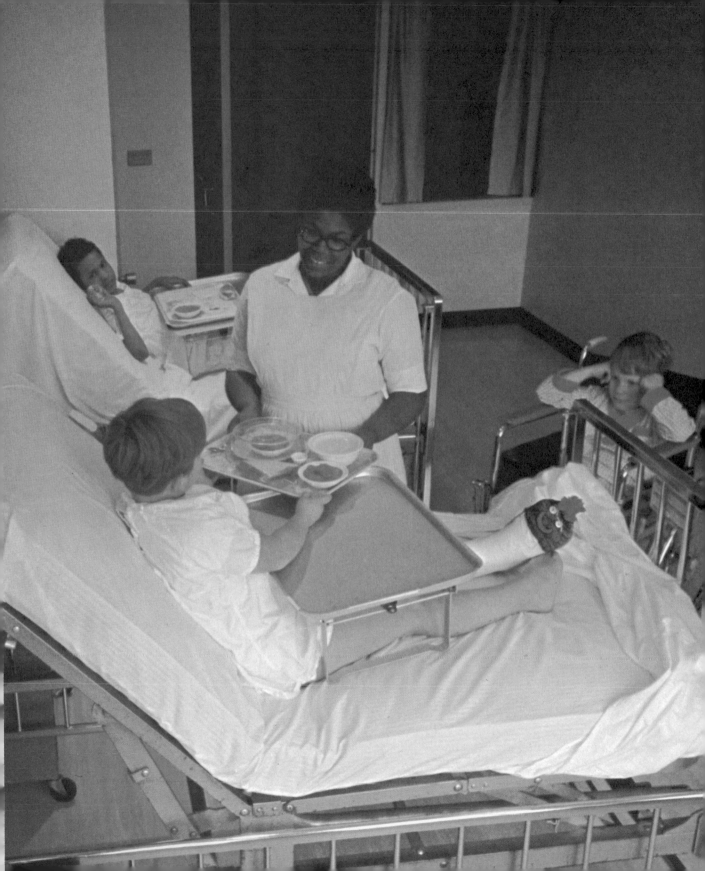

Who Visited Bobby?

Later that morning a woman came with books and toys. Bobby took a book to read.

Before he knew it, it was lunchtime. And then it was naptime.

After the nap, Dr. Zack came to see Bobby. Then his mother came to visit.

After supper, Daddy came to see him.

"Well, Bobby," said Daddy, "the doctor says you can go home soon.

"You can see Dr. Zack at his office from time to time. And before long, you can go back to school."

Bobby said, "I can't wait to tell my friends about the hospital."

What will he tell them?

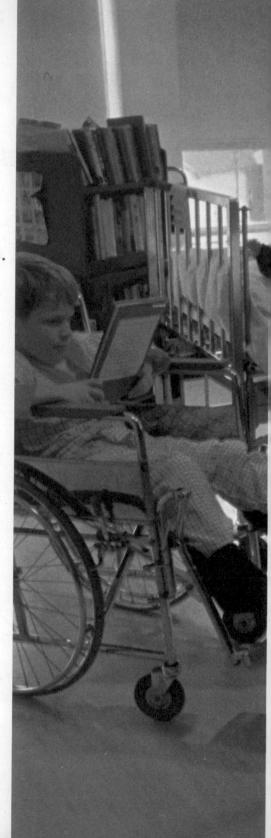

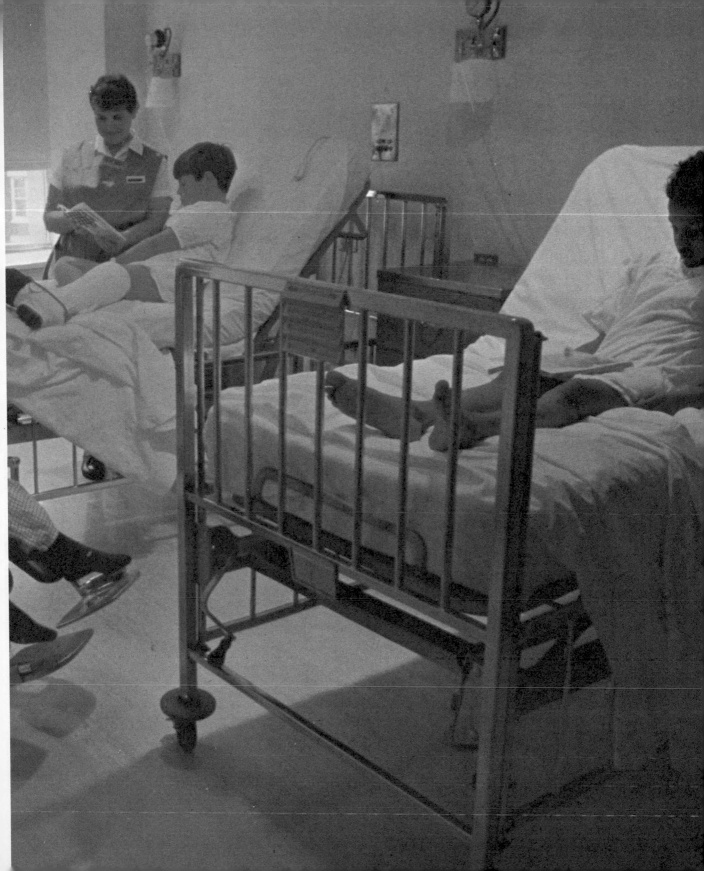

Activities

Teacher's Notes
The book *At the Pet Hospital* is by
Jane Hefflefinger and Elaine Hoffman
(Childrens Press). *Animal Doctors:
What They Do* is by Carla Greene
(Harper). Still another book children
enjoy is *I Know An Animal Doctor* by
Chika A. Iritani (Putnam).
See if children know another name for
a doctor who takes care of animals.
(Veterinarian.) Point out that a
veterinarian may be a man or a woman.

Things to Do

1. Tell what kind of hospital you see here.

2. Tell what we call the doctor who takes care of animals.

3. Tell what is happening in each picture. Or write a sentence or so about a picture you like.

4. Look for books about animal hospitals. Two books you may like are *At the Pet Hospital* and *Animal Doctors: What They Do.*

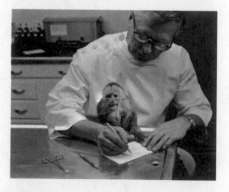

Can You Show What You Know?

Teacher's Notes
Here behavioral objectives in the cognitive area are posed in childlike language directly to the children themselves. In turn, boys and girls give evidence by *observable behavior* of what they have learned.
Other hoped-for objectives lie chiefly in the affective area which is less easily observed. Such objectives pertain to feelings, attitudes, and values. Some of them are:
Is aware of the need for hospitals and of how hospitals can help people.
Realizes that a hospital has many different kinds of workers with special skills.
Discovers what life in a hospital can be like.
Asks questions about hospital routines.
Shows interest in the work of the veterinarian.
See page T40.

1. Tell about some things you would see in a hospital.

2. Tell what you know about X-ray pictures.

3. Name some hospital workers.

4. Tell what happens when blood is taken in a blood test.

5. Tell what a boy or girl might enjoy at a hospital.

6. Tell what you know about an operating room.

7. Draw something that happened to Bobby at the hospital.

8. Draw something you might see at an animal hospital.

Behavioral objectives in the cognitive area are stated here directly to children themselves.

Yes or No?

Teacher's Notes

This "Yes or No?" exercise is a simple test. Have pupils read each question silently and be ready to tell the answer. Or, if the children are able, they might write on their papers each number and after it the correct answer, *yes* or *no*. Then discuss why each answer was chosen.

Answers to the questions are:
1. yes; 2. yes; 3. yes; 4. yes; 5. no;
6. yes; 7. yes; 8. yes; 9.yes.

1. Do you see nurses at a hospital?

2. Do you see doctors at a hospital?

3. Can an X-ray picture show bones?

4. Do some people eat in bed at a hospital?

5. Does an animal doctor take care of people?

6. Does a cast help keep a broken bone in place?

7. Are there books and toys for children who stay at a hospital?

8. Can mothers and fathers visit their children at a hospital?

9. Is there an operating room at a hospital?

SCHOOL & HOME

Teacher's Notes
Let volunteers act out scenes in which they are telling family members about a hospital.
Later provide time for youngsters to report on information gained from the family about hospitals in their community.

Pretend you fell and broke your arm. You have to go to the hospital. How will you act it out?

Tell your family about the hospital.

Ask these questions at home: *Is there a hospital in our town? Where is it? What is its name?*

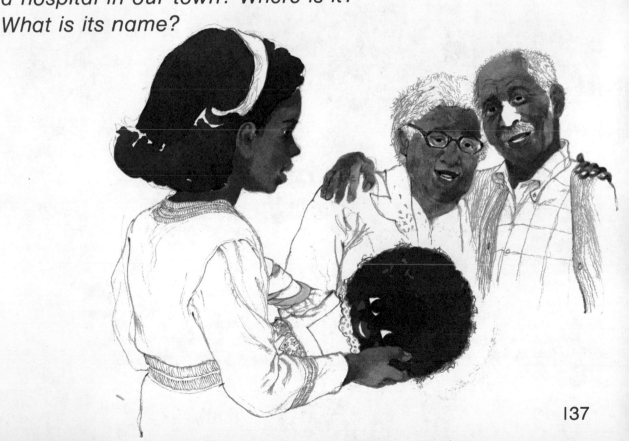

5 About You and Your World

Can you help make things better
in the world around you?
What can you and your family do?

Teacher's Notes
Use the questions on these chapter
title pages to explore youngsters' ideas
of what *they* can do to improve life in
the world around them.
See the Enrichment Suggestions for
Chapter Five on pages T41–T42. See
also the Reference Materials on pages
T45–T46.
Vocabulary Development Introduce
the Words to Know: *electricity,
paper, water, trash, litter, pollute,
noise.* Other words used in Chapter
5 are *bug spray, clean, pollution,
save.*

Words to Know
electricity
litter
noise
paper
pollute
trash
water

How Can You Help?

Every day you decide about some things.

You can decide to make things better. How will you decide?

Teacher's Notes
An attempt is made in this chapter to develop an attitude of personal responsibility on the part of pupils. To make the material more compelling, real-life problems are presented for consideration and decision making.
What Should You Do About the TV?
Have pupils read the text and study the pictured problem. Then have pupils turn the page and check their answers. See also page T41 for additional teaching suggestions.

What Should You Do About the TV?

Suppose you are looking at TV. You decide to go out to play. What should you do before you go out to play?

Now turn the page.

The answer: Turn off the TV.

When you are not using a TV or a radio, turn it off.

Radios and TVs use electricity to make them run.

So turn them off when you are done with them.

That saves electricity.

What other ways can you save electricity?

One way: Turn it off when it is not needed.

Teacher's Notes
The answer: Ask pupils to define electricity—energy that makes appliances, and so on run. See if youngsters can think of other ways to save electricity. (Turn off lights in rooms that are not in use; close refrigerator and freezer doors quickly, so that warm air won't get in and require use of extra electricity to cool the appliances.)
Explain that electricity is not saved only for the sake of saving money, but so we all will have enough to use.
What Should You Do About a Paper Waster?
Have pupils study the text here and picture on page 143 and suggest tentative answers before they turn the page.

What Should You Do About a Paper-Waster?

Suppose you are watching your brother draw.

He starts pictures and then throws them away.

What should you do?

Now turn the page.

The answer: Show your brother
how to save paper.

Help him finish a picture.
Tell him to use both sides of
the paper

Paper is made from trees. The
more paper we use, the more trees
must be cut down.

We need those trees in the world.
What other ways are there
to save paper?

One way: Use paper things again.

Teacher's Notes
The answer: Invite ideas of other ways
to save paper. (Save paper shopping
bags and grocery bags and take them
to the store to be used again; save old
newspapers and take them to collection
places—from there they will go to
factories to be made into *recycled
paper* that can be used again; share
comic books and magazines with
others instead of throwing them away;
and so on.)
Ask:
"What difference does it make whether
or not we waste paper?" (In addition
to saving trees by saving paper, we can
also save money. Each sheet of paper
and each bag costs money.)
How Much Water Do You Need?
Again, invite preliminary discussion of
the problem before the page is turned.
See also page T41.

How Much Water Do You Need?

Suppose you are going to take
a bath.
The tub will hold a lot of water.
How much water will you use?

Now turn the page.

The answer: Use as little water as you can.

Learn to save water.

Then we will all have enough water to use.

What other ways can you save water?

One way: Don't let water run and run.

Teacher's Notes
The answer: Discuss other ways of helping save water. For example, don't let water run while you brush your teeth or wash your face or hands; wash the car by using a bucket of water and a sponge, instead of running water from a hose; be sure to turn water faucets completely off so there won't be dripping; and so on.
What Should You Do with Picnic Trash? Allow ample time for discussing the situation here. Then have pupils turn the page.
See page T42.

What Should You Do With Picnic Trash?

Suppose your family has had a picnic in the park.

It is time to go home.

What should your family do before you go?

Now turn the page.

The answer: Clean up the picnic table. Put the trash in the trash can.

Don't leave litter on the table.

Don't leave litter on the ground.

Keep picnic places clean for others to use.

What else can you do to keep places clean?

One way: Use the town trash baskets to keep streets clean.

Teacher's Notes
The answer: Ask pupils how they would feel if they came to a park for a picnic and the only table available was surrounded by papers, cans, old bottles, and the like. Comment: "What would you do?" (Emphasize that thoughtful people clean up the litter even though they did not make it.)
Where Do You Put the Paper Towel? Mention that sometimes children at school do some littering. Invite comments about where and how this might take place. (Around the wastebasket, in school halls, on the playground, and so on.) Also have the problem situation discussed briefly before the page is turned.
See also page T42.

Where Do You Put the Paper Towel?

Suppose you are in the washroom at school.

You have used a paper towel.

What do you do with it?

Now turn the page.

The answer: Put the paper towel in the trash basket.

Don't drop it on the floor.
How else can you help?
One way: Wipe up spilled water.
Another way: Turn off faucets in the washroom.

Teacher's Notes
The answer: Suggest that pupils check the washrooms at their school for signs of litter. Ask:
"What will you do if you find paper towels on the floor?" (Put them in the wastebasket.)
Talk over, too, why spilled liquids in the washroom, in the kitchen, or in other rooms should be wiped up at once.
What Should You Do About a Fly? Help youngsters with the word *flyswatter* and *bug spray*. Explain that a bug, or insect, spray is a chemical used to kill flies and other insect pests. Then have children read the problem situation and briefly discuss it.
See also page T42.

What Should You Do About a Fly?

Suppose a fly buzzes and buzzes around you.
Should someone get a flyswatter?
Should someone get a bug spray?
What should be done?

Now turn the page.

The answer: Use a flyswatter.

Bug sprays can be dangerous.
They pollute the air.
Only grown-ups should decide
when to use bug sprays.
Then only a *little* should be used.
You can stop flies from coming in.
How can you do this?
One way: Keep the door closed.

Teacher's Notes
The answer: Explain that the danger of bug sprays, such as those used to kill flies, is that people may breathe in too much of them. Bug sprays breathed in can be harmful to health. The warning on the containers usually warns that they should be used in ventilated places. It is important to stress, too, that insect sprays are often used when a better alternative which does not harm the environment could be used— for example, when a flyswatter could do just as well. What is more, bug sprays are poisons and should not be used by children. Also, sprays should be stored where little children cannot get them.
How Should You Play a Radio? Children are sure to have ideas about what's wrong in the situation outlined here. Discuss youngsters' ideas before the page is turned.
See also page T42.

How Should You Play a Radio?

Suppose you have a little radio.
You like to play it.
You turn it up as loud as you can.
How should you play the radio?

Now turn the page.

The answer: Keep the radio turned down.

Loud noise can hurt people's ears.
It makes people feel tired and cross.
Noise can hurt your ears too.
What other things can you do
to cut down on noise?

One way: Keep the TV from playing
too loudly.

Other ways: Try not to slam doors.
Talk; don't shout.

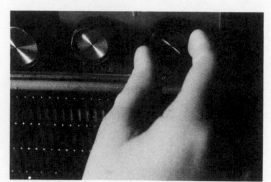

Teacher's Notes
The answer: Talk over the harmful effects of too much noise. Also see if pupils can suggest other things that can be done to cut down on noise. (Keep record players tuned low; don't drag your feet across the floor; don't bang locker doors at school; and so on.) Expand the discussion to include comments on sounds children *like* to hear, on lonely sounds, on happy sounds, on sounds that are unpleasant, and so on.

JUST WRITE

Read what some children wrote about noise and litter.

What can you write?

Teacher's Notes
Give youngsters a chance to write about such topics as "Too Much Noise," "What I Can Do About Litter," "Saving Water," and so on. Pictures might be drawn to accompany the writings.

Noise

I hate too much noise.
It is awful. It hurts my head.
Lisa

Litter

We had a litter hunt.
I found 3 gum wrappers
and someone's spelling paper.
Paul

HEALTH AROUND US

Every day we use lots of water.
Look at the pictures.
What do they show about ways
we use water?
Do you know other ways?

Teacher's Notes
These pages stress the importance of
conserving our water supplies by
helping youngsters visualize the many
ways in which we all use water. (If
our water supplies should ever be
exhausted, we would all be in real
trouble!) Some other uses for water
are for fighting fires, for cooling some
machinery in factories, for cooking.
Ask youngsters:
"In what ways have *you* used water
today?"
"In what ways have you seen others
around you use water today?"
See also page T42.

Do you know why we should not
waste water?
We could not get along without it.

Activities

Teacher's Notes
Discuss what *pollution* means. (It means that something has been made dirty, untidy, ugly, or bothersome.) Some other words, important in consumer health and environmental health, that youngsters might learn to spell are: *noise, litter, water, paper, electricity*.
Another environmental problem that might be considered is litter thrown from *cars*. Ask children if they have ever seen people throw candy wrappers, soft-drink bottles or cans, paper boxes, and so on from cars onto the street or onto people's yards. Invite suggestions about things that can discourage this practice.

Things to Do

1. Here is an important word to know.
   Try to read it.
   Try to write it.
   Learn how to spell it.

pollution

2. Look in the wastebasket at school.
   See if you find signs that someone
   has wasted some paper.

3. Look around you on the playground today.
   See if you find some litter.
   What will you do about it?

4. Draw a picture of how you have used
   water today.

Can You Show What You Know?

Teacher's Notes
Here behavioral objectives in the cognitive area are posed in childlike language directly to the pupils themselves. In turn, boys and girls give evidence by *observable behavior* of what they have learned. Other hoped-for behavioral objectives lie chiefly in the less easily observed affective area. These goals pertain to feelings, attitudes, and values. Some of them are:

Is aware of the need to conserve water and electricity.

Is alert to ways to save paper.

Realizes the need to keep recreation areas tidy.

Cooperates in helping keep school washrooms neat and clean.

Realizes that pesticides are to be used sparingly and by adults.

Is sensitive to how excess noise can affect others.

See also page T42.

1. Tell some ways you can save electricity.

2. Tell some ways you can help save paper.

3. Tell some ways you can help save water.

4. Draw a picture of how to keep things clean and tidy in the school washroom.

5. Draw a picture that shows what to do with litter.

6. Act out a good way to get rid of a fly.

7. Tell what is wrong with too much noise.

8. Name four or five ways people use water.

Behavioral objectives in the cognitive area are stated here directly to children themselves.

Yes or No?

Teacher's Notes
This "Yes or No?" exercise is a simple test. Have pupils read each question silently and be ready to tell the answer. Or, if children are able, they might write on their papers each number and after it the correct answer, *yes* or *no*.
Answers to the questions are:
1. yes; 2. yes; 3. no; 4. yes; 5. no; 6. no; 7. no; 8. yes; 9. yes.
See page T42.

1. Should you turn off the TV set when no one is using it?

2. Is paper made from trees?

3. Should you take a bath with the tub as full as full can be?

4. Should you try to save paper?

5. Should you throw paper towels on the floor in the school washroom?

6. Should you throw cans, bottles, and boxes on the ground?

7. Should people use lots and lots of bug spray?

8. Should you wipe up water you spill?

9. Can loud noises bother people?

SCHOOL & HOME

Teacher's Notes
Special efforts are made in this book and all the books in this series to foster school-home communication and participation.
Parents may be very pleased to note evidences that their youngsters are interested in helping save paper, water, and electricity!
Plan to allot time later for children to report back to the group interesting information gained from parent discussions.
See also page T42.

Tell your family some of the things you have learned. Tell about saving water and paper and electricity.

See if your family knows other ways to help save these things.

Maybe your family will show you electricity or water bills.

You can learn to save electricity and water. That way you can save money too.

Do You Use What You Know?[1]

Teacher's Notes
This is an end-of-the-book review *with special emphasis on how children are applying their health and safety knowledge in daily life.* A notable feature of this review is the provision for children to look back to pages in the book that can tell them things they need to know, in case they have forgotten. The review should facilitate a transfer of important health and safety ideas from the book to everyday life.

1. Have you shown kindness to someone lately?
   What did you do? (18-19)
2. Have you made a mistake lately?
   What did you learn from it? (20-21)
3. Have you felt unhappy or worried lately?
   What did you do about your feelings? (29)
4. How do you keep safe around strange dogs? (48-51)
5. How do you keep safe on a bicycle? (52-55)
6. What do you do if you need to take medicine? (60-63)
7. What kinds of food do you try to eat each day? (79-85)
8. Did you get enough sleep last night? (88-89)
9. What did you do yesterday to get exercise? (90-91)
10. What do you do after you use the washroom? (98-99)
11. What do you do when you watch TV? (102-103)
12. How do you brush your teeth? (106-107)
13. What do you do to save paper? (144)
14. How do you help keep the washroom at school clean?
    (150)

[1]This is an end-of-book review, with emphasis on application of health and safety ideas in daily life. Numbers refer to pages where ideas being reviewed are presented.

Some Health and Safety Words to Know

1 About You

angry

feelings

happy

kind

kindness

mistake

proud

special

unhappy

2 About Your Senses and Your Safety

bicycle

brain

fire

hear

medicine

messages

nerves

safety

see

senses

sign

smell

taste

touch

3 About Your Health Questions

bones

bread

breakfast

cereal

dental hygienist

dentist

doctor

energy

exercise

food

fruit

grow

healthy

joints
meat
milk
muscles
nurse
permanent
primary
six-year molars
skeleton
sleep
teeth
toilet
vegetable
wash

4 About the Hospital

animal
blood
cast
emergency

hospital
laboratory
operating
pulse
recovery
temperature
X-ray

5 About You and Your World

bug spray
clean
electricity
litter
noise
paper
pollute
pollution
save
trash
water

164

Index of Health and Safety Ideas[1]

[1]Major headings refer to the eleven strands in the YOU AND YOUR HEALTH Program.

About the Book

Acknowledgments

YOU AND YOUR HEALTH is especially designed for seven- to eight-year-old children. It centers around the special health and safety needs and interests of this age group.

To facilitate successful use of this book by the children for whom it is particularly intended, much attention has been given to making the text highly readable.

Photographs and illustrations on these pages—26, 34-35, 36-37, 38-39, 40-41, 42-43, 44-45, 46-47, 49, 50-51, 57, 76-77, 78, 81, 82, 83, 84, 85, 88-89, 92, 93, 94, 95, 98-99, 100-101, 104-105, 116-117, 118-119, 120-121, 122-123, 124-125, 126-127, 128-129, 130-131, 132-133, 134—Copyright © 1971, 1974 by Scott Foresman and Company. Cover—Robert Amft.

Appreciation is expressed to the pupils and staffs of the following schools for their cooperation during the photographing of many of the situations pictured in the book: Martin Luther King, Jr., Laboratory School and Miller School, District 65, Evanston, Illinois.

Appreciation is expressed to the staff of Children's Memorial Hospital, Chicago, Illinois for their cooperation in photographing the situations pictured on pages 116-133.